*F*orgiving
the
*U*nforgivable

Forgiving the Unforgivable

BEVERLY FLANIGAN

MACMILLAN • USA

Macmillan General Reference
A Simon & Schuster Macmillan Company
1633 Broadway
New York, NY 10019-6785

Library of Congress Cataloging-in-Publication Data
Flanigan, Beverly.
    Forgiving the unforgivable / Beverly Flanigan. — 1st Collier
Books ed.
        p. cm.
    Includes bibliographical references and index.
    ISBN 0-02-032230-5
    1. Forgiveness. I. Title.
[BF637.F67F53 1994]
158'.2—dc20   93-34336   CIP

First Collier Books Edition 1994

10 9 8 7 6

Printed in the United States of America

Grateful acknowledgment is made for permission to quote from "When Time Is Stolen" by Joan Baez (© 1971, Chandos Music).

CONTENTS

PREFACE

This book presents a construct of forgiving that I believe is both theoretically sound and empowering for those who attempt to use it to forgive people who have harmed them. I do not view the material presented as a substitute for professional therapy but as a companion to it if people need additional help.

It is my sincerest hope that those of you who use this work to help you forgive the unforgivable are able to complete the journey of forgiveness if you choose to attempt it. I am told by all who have done so that the final destination is worth the trip.

Forgiving the Unforgivable was spawned from a lifelong interest in the problems people experience and the methods they use to resolve them. I am sure this interest evolved from my family's commitment to people and their passion for inquiry. I thank them for these. I also want to thank my friends, who have given me their unswerving support during the preparation of the book.

My most special thanks go to all of the people who volunteered their stories of forgiving. Their names have been altered to protect their identities, but their experiences reveal the determination of the human spirit when it refuses to be broken by adversity. To all of you, I am deeply grateful.

Forgiving the Unforgivable could not have been realized without the support of the Kellogg Foundation and my agent, Jane Jordan Browne, the constructive comments of my editor, Natalie Chapman, and the expert assistance of Betty Zeps.

Forgiving
the
Unforgivable

Introduction

My interest in forgiveness began many years ago, when I was a young social worker in Alaska. I was working with an adolescent girl who had witnessed her father murder her mother. The girl had also been raped by her father. Although many seasoned helping professionals have faced this situation fairly often, I was confronted for the first time with a client who, regardless of the evidence that lay before her about her father's behavior and character, struggled determinedly to forgive him. Also for the first time, I was in a deep quandary about whether to help someone reach for an objective with which I was not certain I agreed.

When I left full-time clinical practice to teach, questions about clients who wanted to reconcile with people who hurt them persisted; so did my students' questions about the ultimate purposes of the helping process. Should people who are abused by their parents simply reject their own mothers and fathers? Should they express their rage toward others? For how long? What is enough? Should they break their vows of fidelity because their spouses become cruel or ill? Is the goal of "empowering" a person to assist that individual in placing blame on another? My fascination with the underlying value of helping others and with the goals of helping continued to spur me to attempt to find answers to these questions, mostly because I strongly suspected that the goals clients had for themselves were often not those of helping professionals.

Many people, whether professionals understand it or not, seem to need to make things right with each other when things have gone wrong between them. Forgiveness is one mechanism for righting wrongs. Over the course of my work, I have come to suspect that there are many more people than we can imagine waiting to hear the words "I forgive you" or "Please forgive me" so that they can finally feel at peace with the people they have once loved.

If a group of average people were asked the question "When you review your life, what one thing about it still makes you feel bad?" the answer for many would involve forgiving. Some would feel bad because they had been unable to forgive another; some, because they had not been forgiven by a person for whom they had once cared. Forgiveness is the method by which people in intimate relationships let each other "off the hook" for various acts of ruthlessness and unkindness. It is the figurative glue that holds together intimate bonds. But it is elusive; and remaining unforgiven or unforgiving is an all-too-common fate for countless individuals. Forgiving is among the most difficult of human undertakings; unfortunately, most of us have no idea how to forgive each other or even if we should attempt to do so.

Very little is actually known about forgiving and how it happens. In fact, more is written about the results of forgiving than about the process itself. For example, the end product of forgiveness is that it presumably repairs ruptures between people.[1] It is said to release those who injure others from paying off a debt, whether the debt is material or emotional. Forgiveness allows the forgiven to start all over as though his* slate of old behaviors were wiped clean.[2] It is said to be permanent; that is, once given, it cannot be retracted.[3] But such observations shed little light on what it is—on what actually goes on in the hearts and minds of people who have been deeply wounded and who have struggled to forgive the person who did the wounding. In 1982, I set out to find some answers about the experience of forgiving the unforgivable.

From 1980 through 1983, I was fortunate enough to have been a fellow of the Kellogg Foundation (one of the largest philanthropic foundations in the country). As part of my fellowship, I decided to return to the classroom to audit some courses. In a doctoral seminar I attended one afternoon, the students were entertaining several questions: Are moral people required to forgive? Their answer was yes. Are they required to forgive even a tyrant like Rudolf Hess (who was still living in Spandau at the time)? Again, their answer was yes.

The logic behind the students' consensus was that when tyrants act in injurious ways, they engender in the broader society the likelihood that hatred seething in victims of tyranny spills out in ever-widening spheres of influence onto nonvictims and eventually everyone connected with nonforgiveness. The hateful recriminations of a victim, their logic went, are as morally dangerous as the acts of the tyrant. Each one, the victim or the villain, is likely to contribute to a society's evolution into a crueler place. Regardless of its source, hatred creates meanspiritedness in the human condition. So when an individual does not forgive one who injures him, he perpetuates evil and, in the end, affects the well-being of everyone. Forgiving, by this logic, is the only ethical response to villainy.

The problem, though, was that forgiveness was never well defined. If people have a duty to forgive, what exactly *is* forgiving? I began to examine other sources of information and, to my surprise, found that little is actually known about the subject. I scoured the literature, reexamined the philosophies of twelve-step groups (like Alcoholics

---

* Because both men and women forgive their injurers, masculine and feminine pronouns will be used in alternate chapters throughout the remainder of the book.

Anonymous), and talked with other professionals. Finally, with the financial assistance of the Kellogg Foundation, I designed a study to pursue a logical course. I decided to interview people who had "forgiven the unforgivable." To find individuals willing to talk about such difficult personal matters as unforgivable offenses, I placed ads in newspapers in six sites around the United States (and in New Zealand for comparison). Over the next two and a half years, I traveled to meet and talk with seventy respondents, each of whom had forgiven something he'd at first considered unforgivable. I met people in their homes, restaurants, city parks, or wherever else they felt free to talk. I heard stories of murders, unfaithfulness, lies, betrayals, abandonment, and viciousness, sometimes almost beyond belief. Each interviewee was audiotaped; and each tape was played and replayed until its contents could be analyzed. Slowly and surely, specific themes began to emerge. The experiences of the people I met are interwoven throughout this book. You will meet them as their words reveal the complex and profound nature of forgiveness.

From the study that forms the basis of much of this book and the many workshops I have presented on forgiving, along with twenty years of research, discussion with colleagues, clinical practice, and teaching students the art of helping, a theory of forgiving has developed. Before I discuss it, though, more needs to be said about human nature and the many ways we injure each other. Some injuries fall into the category "unforgivable"; some do not.

The singular characteristic that distinguishes human beings from all other species is that we knowingly and often without legitimate reason cause each other to suffer. We lie to each other, cheat each other, rape each other, pummel and abandon each other, humiliate each other, and betray each other. Even more peculiar, we most often do these things not to our enemies but to the people closest to us.

Human groups have always engaged in wars with enemies. Wars give groups the sanction to inflict violence on each other. Wars also create an environment in which one individual can find justification for causing another individual to suffer. But the vast amount of human suffering does not occur between warring groups on battlefields. Most of it takes place in a different war zone—between individuals in intimate relationships. Unlike injury in war, where hate precipitates violence, injuries between intimates are spawned from a mixture of love and other emotions. Whereas hate causes violence and hardens hearts, love precipitates injuries that break them. Unforgivable injuries are the injuries of intimate people. When they happen, hearts are broken, and the essence of intimacy is destroyed. So, the worst kind of human wounds occur not on battlefields but in our homes. The worst injurers are not enemies or strangers in a foxhole but our husbands and wives, children, parents, and friends. Wherever love has been a part of relationships, the shrapnel of human destruction is strewn in our living rooms and bedrooms in the form of aborted dreams and wounded hopes. Wars may terminate with the signing of peace treaties, but intimate injuries have no such formal mechanisms for ending them. The most intimate of injuries are often left festering and unresolved—either unforgiven or unforgivable.

Forgiving is not the same as pardoning.[4] Pardoning releases people from punishments due them and usually is the result of the act of a person in authority. A governor pardons a prisoner, for example.[5] Forgiveness, on the other hand, takes place between intimates; it does not possess the objectivity of pardoning.

Forgiveness has nothing to do with forgetting, either. A wounded person cannot—indeed, should not—think that a fading memory can provide an expiation of the past. To forgive, one must remember the past, put it into perspective, and move beyond it. Without remembrance, no wound can be transcended.

Forgiveness is also not accomplished through pronouncement. The words "I forgive you" may be appropriate to minor, everyday accidents or social indiscretions, but if real damage has resulted between people, no mere words can effect significant repair.[6]

The one enduring idea about what forgiveness actually is (rather than what it is not) is reiterated in a common theme in the literature written about it. Forgiving is said to occur in a *transaction*.[7] This transaction takes place between two parties—the offended person and the offender. It is supposedly an orderly series of exchanges that results in the repair of a ruptured relationship. The "transactional model" of forgiving occurs in the following sequence: First, the injured accuses his injurer. Next, the injurer steps forward and admits that he caused another person harm; then he not only helps but encourages the wounded person to express his own feelings—even if they are of rage. The injurer then accepts the wrongness of his actions and takes punishment if need be.[8] He promises never to repeat his offense. There is an outpouring of emotion on the part of both individuals—guilt, sorrow, anger, and finally love. The end result is a renewal of commitment to each other and a restoration of what had been a nearly ruptured relationship. As with a cracked vase glued back together, in the ideal model of forgiveness, the relationship is repaired, and the individuals are ready to take on new commitments and burdens.[9]

The "transactional model" of forgiveness is shown in figure 1.

If forgiving occurs in an orderly manner for some people, a larger question becomes, how often does it actually take place? How applicable is the model to late-twentieth-century life in the United States? The answer I learned is, not very often.

For a transaction to occur between people, two essential elements are needed: Both people must be present to participate; and both must be *willing* to do so. For many people who have been hurt by those they have loved, this is simply not the situation. Most people forgive alone, with little or no help from others. The reasons for "solitary forgiving" are several and profoundly reflective of modern life. Changes in the twentieth century have created extraordinary circumstances where human relationships are concerned. Put simply, people—at least, most Americans—do not need each other to assure their survival. Children can leave parents, husbands can abandon wives, and friends need never speak to one another again. American life has made it possible for people to quickly sever their most intimate relationships and to leave behind those closest to them after one has hurt the other. We are a mobile society. We are prideful and competitive. We dislike losers. Many of us believe that forgivers are wimps or that people who stick around to help someone they hurt pick up the pieces are fools. The transaction of forgiving is

Fig. 1 Transactional Model of Forgiveness

INJURED   INJURER

Accuses the injurer of
violating a rule between them. $--\rightarrow$ Apologizes for breaking the
                                                                rule. $_____$

$\leftarrow_____$

Summarizes the reasons the
injurer's actions were wrong. $--\rightarrow$ Listens and accepts.

$\leftarrow_____$

Expresses rage, sorrow. Feels re-
morse. Punishes the injurer. $--\rightarrow$ Accepts this punishment.

$\leftarrow_____$

Seeks assurance the injury
will not be repeated. $--\rightarrow$ Promises to never repeat
                                                                the injury.

$\leftarrow_____$

Accepts promises and demands no
further payment. $--\rightarrow$ Trusts that forgiveness is
                                                                permanent.

impossible when one party is unwilling or unavailable to talk to the other.

Modern society mitigates the necessity for reconciliation between warring factions or ruptured relations. This has not always been the case.

In primitive societies and in centuries past people had to rely on each other. Members of tribes or clans depended on one another to meet their most basic needs. Procurement of food, clothing, shelter, and safety was impossible without the cooperative efforts of each member. Each individual played a role essential to the survival of the whole. The loss of one person threatened the survival of all.

In hunting-and-gathering cultures, for example, each person—the hunter, gatherer, cook, caretaker of children, wise elder, and even the tribal historian—was essential to the well-being of the community. Fortunately or unfortunately, in contemporary Western culture, the mutual dependence of individuals has broken down. Today it is conceivable that an individual (an adult, at least) could exist entirely alone. He could go to the store for food and clothing, rely on his TV or VCR for entertainment, and do his work at a computer terminal in his condo. Interdependence at an interpersonal level has ceased to exist. Conceivably, a man or woman could work, eat, sleep, and die alone—cut off from all but the social and business institutions that meet his basic needs for food and shelter.

In primitive times, when one member offended another, it was essential that some mechanism for reconciling the injury was present. An errant member had to be allowed to return to the clan to ensure its survival, independent of the survival of the individual. No one could survive totally alone, and the group could not afford to lose any member.*

Forgiveness, apart from being a mechanism for mending ruptured relationships between two individuals, was a method of restoring peace to the human groups to which individuals belong.[10] It was a stopgap that prevented the injuries between individuals from becoming hostilities between their families and prevented family hostilities from becoming wars between their clans. In that way, forgiveness was a mechanism of survival not only for those who

---

* Among the pygmies in Africa, for example, an errant member was required to leave the village and go into the forest alone. He was, for a time, completely ostracized. No one spoke to him at all. The whole village discussed and reviewed his offense. After several days, the ostracized offender quietly and simply walked back into the village, uttering not a word until a designated child took him a bowl of food. The giving of food symbolically represented forgiveness by all members of the group and a willingness to reaccept the offender. Reacceptance assured his, and their, continued survival. In fact, the element of giving something tangible is often a part of a forgiving ritual and symbolizes the idea that reacceptance of those who harm others is itself a gift given by one person to another (C. Trumbull, *The Forest People* [New York: Simon and Schuster, 1962], pp. 102–17).

depended on each other for their personal needs but also for those who were at odds with each other to begin with. Forgiveness prevented the spread of hatred.

Today we are less mutually dependent as individuals, couples, friends, neighbors, or communities. People can do without each other and move in and out of any or all of these human groups as often as they like. The wounded individual grapples alone, and the injurer can move on to other partnerships, friendships, neighborhoods, and communities, carrying with him only the baggage of past relationships. But this does not mean that people do not *need* to feel the peace that forgiveness brings. It means that it has gotten much harder to forgive.

Agents of Forgiveness

In the past as well as the present, churches and synagogues have been thought of as institutions of mercy, reparation, and expiation. The church, of all societal institutions, is linked with compassion and reconciliation. People who seek to forgive or to be forgiven might turn to their pastor, priest, or rabbi for help. But the clergy, even though they are church leaders, are also as involved with the technological and mobile modern scene as anyone else. When a clergyman is asked to help someone forgive an injurer, he may know neither the offended nor the offender. He can only second-guess why the harm occurred. The church, like other sectors of society, suffers from impersonalism and size; and those who would turn to it for help in forgiving are often confronted by that reality.

Others expected to foster forgiveness are members of the professional "helping community." Psychologists, social workers, family therapists, and psychiatrists all work with clients for whom forgiving is a central issue. Professional training, however, rarely focuses on forgiveness as a goal in therapeutic intervention with clients. As a matter of fact, quite the contrary is often true. The therapeutic community—at least some facets of it—holds that "empowerment" or venting of anger is a major and most desirable end state of therapy.

As a rule of thumb, most helping professionals believe that if a client comes to think more positively about himself, improvement will take place in his relationships with others. So, therapy involves self-improvement and the learning of self-improvement techniques (assertion, relaxation, claiming one's feelings, and so on). The therapeutic "graduate" may be able to function and over time may feel his wound less acutely. Deep inside, however, the residual effects of the injury may continue to poison him in the form of mistrust of others or misplaced anger. (Some people fly into fits of rage years after they have been injured at the simple mention of their offender's name.) Wrongs righted in the self do not right wrongs between people who harm each other; they remain in silent places, waiting for the transaction of forgiveness and the relief it bears.

What do people who need to forgive an injurer actually do to heal their hearts? If therapists or clergy are not helpful, what recourse does a wounded person have? There are three ways to end a growing skirmish on a battlefield: raise a white flag of surrender, retreat in defiance, or fight to the bloody end. The same is true of injuries that occur on the battlefield at home. People can forswear their intractable positions and retreat; they can forgive; or when a method of forgiveness is unavailable, they can fight to the end.

The courtrooms in America are teeming with wounded and furious people. Acrimonious divorces, bitter custody feuds, and even small claims between friends are the order of the day in our litigious society. The legal system is one that forces face-to-face combat between an injured person and his injurer. When offenders can walk away from those they harm, the injured can exert what remaining control they have by forcing a confrontation with their injurers in courts of law. When there is no apology, a court case may follow.

In American society, justice and mercy are so closely intertwined that they often are difficult to distinguish. In fact, Judeo-Christian societies are supposed to be prime examples of justice and mercy merged. The unfortunate conclusion might be drawn that whenever mercy is not forthcoming, justice will be sought. If human beings "need" to make things right through forgiveness but are barred from an opportunity to do so, they may seek rightness in the form of "justice."

Forgiving is the method by which the wounded person can readmit an outcast. In forgiving, a wounded person reopens his heart to take in and reaccept his offender. Upon reacceptance, the slate is wiped clean. But it is not possible to readmit someone who is not knocking on the door asking for readmittance; and most injurers not only do not knock at the door but have already opened new doors and stepped through them.

Still, forgiveness is possible to achieve. The reality is that more often than not, forgiveness occurs not as part of a transaction with the injurer but as a result of a solitary process doggedly and painfully pursued by a person who has been badly injured. In other words, forgiveness happens, but it too often happens with no outside help at all.

Unfortunately, an unforgivably wounded person must heal himself. The church or therapists may help, but without the opportunity to confront an offender directly, the offended person must still repair his own heart. Otherwise, he might waste his life waiting for either a chance to face his injurer or an apology that will never come.

The people interviewed for this book healed themselves. They forgave almost every kind of injury—some of them nothing short of heinous. Still, they forgave.

What they experienced in common was a progression through a sequence of phases that helped them to forgive, even though they had to do it alone. It is the "solitary model" of forgiveness and its phases that will be presented here. The ability of human beings to forgive the unforgivable—even if they have to do it alone—is a testament to all that is right about our species. It speaks to the fact that there remains, even in the latter part of the twentieth century, an inner conscience—a need to make things right when people have hurt and been hurt by each other. Forgiveness, whether a mechanism for survival or a basic need of the conscience, nonetheless happens. And when it is final, it imparts peace to the forgiver and restores a modicum of kindness to the human community as a whole.

PART **I**

Anatomy of an Unforgivable Injury

CHAPTER **1**

Anatomy of an
Unforgivable Injury

Forgiveness to the injured does belong.
JOHN DRYDEN, *The Conquest of Granada*

One Wednesday afternoon, Ann Roland drove home from her job as a nurse at the local hospital, just as she had done for the past eight years, expecting to arrive home to an empty house. When she pulled into her driveway, though, a midsized rent-it-yourself moving van was parked there. Ann got out of her car, approached the van, and peered inside. Then she saw her belongings—not all of them, but a television, some chairs, a cardboard wardrobe, boxes of unidentified objects, and even one of her favorite paintings from the living-room wall. Her heart suddenly sank in an eerie and unknown fear.

Ann closed the garage door behind her and walked slowly into the kitchen. From there she saw her husband, Jerry, sitting in one of the chairs that remained in their living room. He looked slowly up at her and, his eyes finally meeting hers, said, "I'm leaving you. It just isn't good anymore, and I guess you'll find out, anyhow. I have another woman. We've been together for three years, and I want to marry her." There was a pause. "I promise I'll send money for the kids." A car honked outside. Jerry looked at Ann. "I've got to go now." He rose and walked toward the front door. Ann stood frozen in her place. Through the living-room window she saw a woman driving Jerry's car. The woman pulled directly up behind the moving van. Jerry opened the door, never looking back, and walked away. He climbed into the van, and the woman started Jerry's car. She pulled out into the street, pointed the car east, and inched into traffic, pausing for Jerry to pull out behind her. That was the last Ann saw of Jerry until their first mediation hearing three months later.

With four sentences, Ann's world fell apart. A contract she thought she had made for life was shredded in front of her face. The contract was not only legal and a public, religious proclamation of honor and fidelity; it involved right and wrong and how people treat each other. It concerned morality and personal integrity. It was a contract steadily hewed out of the events of her life with her husband and a guideline for their future life together. Now all was destroyed. Ann had been unforgivably wounded. And she had only begun to feel the full force of her injury.

Ann Roland would live for many months staggered by her wound, simultaneously feeling sorrow and hatred, confusion and self-blame. She would physically falter, getting sick frequently and losing sleep night after night. She would be unable to concentrate and would subsequently do poorly at her job. Finally, Ann faced the fact that she had been permanently and profoundly changed; she could either forgive her injurer or choose not to. In effect, she could choose to let her husband's infidelity and abandonment govern her life from that moment on or forgive him and go on with her life. The choice would be hers.

What Makes an Injury Unforgivable?

Life is filled with all kinds of personal hurts: white lies, broken promises, even physical injuries, like spankings or maybe an unintentional slap thrown during a lovers' quarrel. Most of the wounds we experience, though, are not unforgivable. We put them behind us and go on. In fact, if we could not do so, our lives would become like scoreboards. People could routinely add up their wounds and demand payment. Or they could keep count of their injuries and match injury for injury, much as they do in more retaliatory societies. If not for forbearance, life would be a never-ending series of tit-for-tat recriminations and acrid reminders of wrongdoings. People could not live for long, at least peacefully, in such a way.

Unforgivable injuries like the one Ann Roland experienced, though, are not like smaller offenses. They cannot simply be put aside or ignored. Injuries like Ann's are also different from burglaries, attacks by muggers, or even rapes by unknown assailants. These damage people, but they do not involve love, and they do not force people to reevaluate their assumptions about love and being loved. Ann's injury permanently changed her, as do all unforgivable injuries.

There are five major characteristics that make an injury unforgivable:

1. Unforgivable injuries start with a singular event that signals a betrayal.
2. They are intitiated by intimate injurers, not strangers.
3. They are moral wounds; they shatter a person's concept of morality.
4. They assault a person's most fundamental belief systems.
5. They are deeply personal and therefore relative from wounded person to wounded person.

The experiences of the people I interviewed make the five characteristics clear.

Carol, a thirty-four-year-old mother:

> *I am divorced. My husband left me on Christmas of 1980. He was in love with a woman ten years younger than me. I think that alone I could have handled it, but the time he chose to leave was impeccably poor. I had breast cancer and at the time was in my third month of chemotherapy. The stress of the whole mess made me violently ill. Now, I haven't gotten to the bad part yet.*
>
> *My ex-husband was terribly cruel throughout the entire affair. He stole all my silver, which were gifts to me. He said he would fight me to death for the boys' custody. In a nutshell, he won. (The courts said I may die and unstabilize the boys. Besides, he could support them. I don't even have a job.)*
>
> *The icing on the cake for all this is that the attorney fee for JUST my part was $18,000. I had to sell the house.*

Dave, a successful contract engineer:

> *I have been separated for ten months from a twenty-four-year-marriage which was, for the most part, miserable. (I am forty-four years old.) During the final eight years preceding the separation, I had a girlfriend (divorced). As my situation worsened and she began to recognize I was going to leave home, she ended our relationship. This to me was an unforgivable act. I feel I have forgiven her completely, but the process was difficult, to put it mildly. My emotions ran the full gamut during this past year.*
>
> *My seventeen-year-old son was stricken with fibrosarcoma the year before. It subsequently metastasized to both lungs, and after six surgical procedures, three months of radiation therapy, and eighteen months of various chemotherapy protocols, he passed away. During his illness, I felt an almost uncontrollable anger, probably fueled by my helplessness in the situation, against God, myself, my wife, my girlfriend, the impotence of the doctors, all healthy people, and the world in general.*

Sarah, nineteen years old:

> *When I was small, my mom died, and my dad remarried about a year after my mom's death. Neither of them wanted me or my three brothers. They spent all their time in taverns. They didn't care about our welfare or our emotional needs. I raised myself until I was fourteen. I was resentful and hated them both very much.*
>
> *They made me and my brothers live down in the basement some of the time. And we weren't allowed to walk on the carpets. We had to walk AROUND them, like a dog. I started to be as bad as they were. I drank and hung around with bad kids. I guess I hated everything, including myself, to the point I wanted to kill myself.*

These experiences arose from different kinds of relationships. Different events signaled the beginning of each injury. But each was unforgivable to the person who described it. Each incorporated all five characteristics. Each involved a betraying event, was spawned from intimacy, was moral in nature, precipitated the loss of deeply held beliefs, and was intensely personal.

These five characteristics are important for would-be forgivers (or their friends and counselors) to understand. If they are not grasped fully, only the most superficial aspects of a wound might be identified, and thus an inaccurately identified offense might be forgiven.

The Betraying Event

In the best circumstances, the relationships between husbands and wives, parents and children, or friends are unlike all others. They germinate in the recognition of mutual attraction, they mature in growing trust and respect, and they flourish in a kind of blind-faith assumption that each person will behave in the other's best interest. In no other relationships can such an assumption be made. Unlike strangers, people who are intimate with each other not only weave their own unique histories of personal events (ups and downs, joys and struggles) but also create a moral history unique only to them.[1]

A moral history is like other histories. It evolves from an accumulation of events; it becomes more complex over time; and it takes on patterns. But a moral history, unlike others, refers to what two people in a relationship develop together as acceptable or unacceptable ways to treat one another. Moral histories are the histories of right and wrong.

Early in marriages or friendships, people begin to establish, for example, whether they will always tell the truth, whether they can borrow an item and not return it, whether they can be late for appointments with each other, or even whether they can have an occasional affair. Partners, children, friends, and parents learn when they will or will not be punished for their behavior. As relationships deepen and become more complex, the definition of acceptable behavior toward each other begins to take form and crystallize. Over time, a truly moral relationship forms. By "moral," I mean that the guiding principles that propel the relationship forward are those that allow both people to aspire to their own ambitions and at the same time set limits to acceptable behavior. In moral relationships, all parties can feel free to maximize their own interests. In fact, each person wants the other to do so. Moreover, one member cannot benefit herself if, in doing so, the action takes something away from the other person. "Moral relationship" does not imply that people always treat each other with total respect or never lie to each other, cheat, or break promises. In fact, it may mean quite the contrary. People may agree to all kinds of behaviors in their relationship that others might judge as unkind or even immoral. The point is that each relationship develops its own moral "rules of the game," whatever they may be, and that the agreements of a relationship require that people stick to the rules, no matter what they are. The continued allegiance to agreed-upon moral rules in any relationship evolves into a moral history between two people, however odd that moral history might appear to others.

Take marital rules of right and wrong, for example, and the wide range of moral rules people adhere to. One couple, the Joneses, agrees early on that each can flirt with other people at social events. In fact,

Mrs. Jones becomes excited when she sees attractive women drawn to her husband. Mr. Jones feels a certain prowess when other men court his wife. After parties, they have their best sex. The Coopers, on the other hand, decide early on in their relationship that flirting is absolutely unacceptable. (They decide this after a flirtation of Mr. Cooper's resulted in the worst fight of their marriage.) To Mr. and Mrs. Cooper, a flirtation is a threat to their happiness and will not be engaged in. If either Mr. or Mrs. Cooper were suddenly to flirt openly again, the event would signal the possible disintegration of the Coopers' current moral agreement with each other.

Friends, parents and children, brothers and sisters, carve out their sets of moral rules through trial and error, crisis and calm. Over time, the moral rules and resulting history of any two people are as unique as a fingerprint.

Moral rules become the foundation of trust between people.[2] Voluntary allegiance to rules of a relationship says, in effect, "I can be I, and you can be you. In being myself, I won't take advantage of you; and in being yourself, you won't take advantage of me. I believe we both want this for ourselves and each other, and I believe we both want to live within the rules of right and wrong we've set for ourselves. I will abide by them, and I know you will." Any relationship with a moral history has thus evolved from trials and errors and the testing and retesting of acceptable limits to behaviors. Although change and evolution are ongoing in a relationship, there is a set of moral rules that currently governs and defines it. Moral rules can best be defined as mutually developed, voluntary agreements between two people that set limits to acceptable behaviors and within which both people can assert their interests without encroaching upon the other's capacity to do the same.[3]

An unforgivable injury begins with an event that violates the current moral rules of a relationship. The event signals that one person no longer complies with what is thought to be right and wrong and instead maximizes her own advantage to the disadvantage of the other person by breaking the relationship's rules. An unforgivable event, no matter what its nature, sets the moral history between two people off on a different course.

Here is an example of how the injury begins.

The manager of a car dealership, Carl, knows that his car salesmen often stretch the truth in order to make a sale. In fact, in sales meetings, the sales staff usually exchange jokes among themselves about various tall tales they've told prospective customers. Each month, Carl gives out the "There's a Sucker Born Every Minute" award to the salesman who employs the most creative scam to sell a car.

Carl is grooming Bill, his favorite young salesman, to become the new sales manager someday. Bill is both Carl's protégé and surrogate son. He has quickly moved up through the ranks to become head salesman and is the envy of all the staff. With Carl's help, Bill has become a master at "doublespeak"; he can lie without flinching. He is a smooth, calculating, almost ruthless businessman, and he is Carl's pride and joy.

One day, Carl learns from a car dealer across town that Bill has interviewed for the position of sales manager with a direct competitor of Carl's dealership and that he will soon take the job. Bill apparently has lied about his credentials, and even his salary, to the competition. Carl is crushed and furious. He confronts Bill with what he has heard, and Bill flatly denies it. Two weeks later, Bill quits and begins his management job the next day at the competitor's dealership.

Carl is devastated. He feels betrayed and victimized, but more than that, stunned. He cannot believe that Bill would deceive him. Deceit is fine in business but absolutely intolerable between friends. So begins Carl's unforgivable wound.

All unforgivable injuries begin with an event that transgresses the moral rule between two people (like Bill's lie to Carl). However, in contrast to other wounds, it does not stop there, whether the event is a lie, an affair, a sexual assault, or the violation of a promise. Events are usually what people speak of as "unforgivable"; but in reality, events represent only a minuscule part of an unforgivable injury. One violation of a moral rule between two people does not constitute an unforgivable injury. What comes after it does.

The Three Pathways of Moral Injuries

When agreements as to what is right and wrong behavior between any two people are violated, the wound can follow one of three pathways (fig. 2). The first two are not unforgivable, but the third one is.

On the first pathway, both people recognize the violation. Both feel bad, but the injurer feels particularly guilty. All the while, though, both continue to believe that the moral agreement between them was and still is a good one. One party made a mistake, that's all. However painful the mistake might be, both people want to adhere again to the original rules they developed together. In fact, on this first pathway, the transactional process of forgiving usually takes place. The contrite member can apologize and make promises. The violated person can in response condemn or even punish the offender. In the end, the apologies are accepted. The anger passes, and both people voluntarily agree to commit themselves to their original moral beliefs as to how they should treat each other. They may even decide to change the rules a little; but both people again agree to live by them. This would have happened between Carl and Bill if Bill had felt contrite, confessed his behavior to Carl, turned down the other job offer, and promised never to betray Carl again. Carl might still be angry, but knowing that Bill is volunteering on his own to pledge himself to their rules of honesty again, he decides nonetheless to take Bill back and to harbor no ill will toward him. Bill's mistake was a fluke.

On the second pathway of moral injury, the same transactional forgiveness process appears to occur, on the surface at least. Instead, though, while both people say they are willing again to comply with the old rules of fairness, one person, without the other's knowing it, decides to live by a new set of rules. A spouse who continues to have affairs after she has promised not to is an example. When this happens, the moral history of two people begins to break off into two separate directions—one person pursuing right and wrong along one road and the other knowing that she is not on the same pathway but is pretending to be. This "low road" is built on pretense, pock-

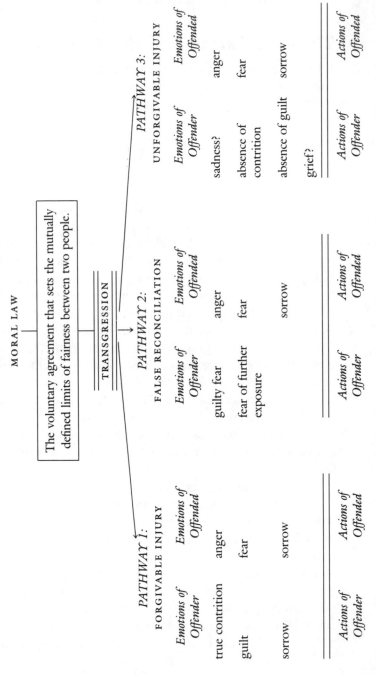

Fig. 2 Three Pathways of Injury

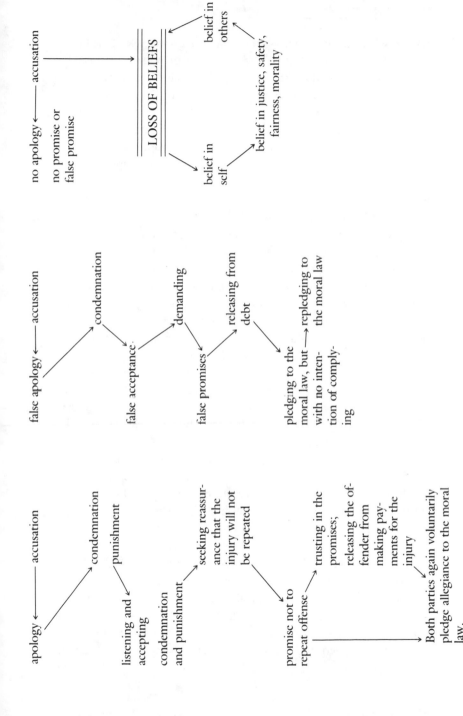

marked with lies, and lined with deceit. If Bill promises Carl he will never betray him again but behind the scenes provides the dealership across town inside information about Carl's sales strategies or methods of cutting costs, Bill is taking the second pathway of moral injury.

This second pathway of injury may continue for the duration of a relationship; but if it does, the relationship is bound to change in several ways. When deceit is at the core of two people's arrangements (whether parents and their children, spouses, or friends), secrets begin to displace any real communication. One person stops sharing her innermost thoughts and feelings with the other, retreating further and further into silence. Intimacy dissolves; or worse yet, is feigned. As the participants go their separate ways (morally at least), emotional nurturance wanes. People may perhaps go through the motions of keeping up pretenses and routines, but the essential element between them—truth—is gone. Relationships of all kinds can go on like this for many years or forever. Often, however, they take the third pathway of moral injury: A betraying event evolves into a full-blown, unforgivable injury and ruptures the relationship between the very people who created their own moral history.

An injury that alters a moral history and ruptures a relationship begins with an event that violates a moral rule but does not stop there. Instead, it spirals on to violate other beliefs of the injured person, destroying in its wake belief after belief until the wounded person, too, is nearly destroyed.

An unforgivable injury is a profound and irreversible assault on the fundamental belief system of the person who has been injured. It is not just the lie but what happens to everything one believed in as a result of the lie that makes the lie so profound. It is not the battering but what happens to a battered woman's beliefs as a result of the battering that makes it unforgivable. It is not even the incest or the infidelity or the abandonment that is unforgivable but the effect such offenses have on everything else the victim either believed in or attempted to believe in that makes it unforgivable. These injuries separate people from the very ideas they once believed were true—beliefs about themselves, the world, other people, good and bad, right and wrong, the future, and even the validity of the history they have shared with the person who hurt them. Unforgivable injuries are injuries to and separations from beliefs. They are a profound disturbance of assumptions. They cause suffering because they separate a person from something treasured.

An unforgivable injury is like a domino toppling a row of other standing dominoes. Once the event occurs, more and more assumptions start to fall. Other unforgivable events may be revealed. Other violations of moral rules may emerge. As the injury expands and widens, the pain of the wounded increases, too. A woman whose marriage crumbled after her husband left her without warning described vividly how her beliefs were shattered:

> *What did I have to believe in anymore if I couldn't believe in a man I had come to know so well? So there was a loss in me of myself. Where had I been all of these years? I felt responsible because I wasn't aware of what was going on. I felt responsible for things I had done in the marriage that caused this. I lost faith in other people because their support was "He was a lousy person; you're lucky." I lost faith in the professions—the world of professional people who were supposed to be there when you needed them. My attorney was a schlock. My first psychologist didn't work. Now I'm a failure; now I can't even find support. So it was tough at times. Everything was gone. And it wasn't because he walked out of my life. Maybe that was the cause. But the effects were the things I was dealing with. He was not the only thing in my life, but it did bring the rest of my world tumbling down.*

The Three Levels of Damaged Beliefs

Unforgivable injuries shatter beliefs at three levels. They shatter the injured person's assumption that the behavior of other people in their lives can be predicted. People lose faith in the loyalty of friends, the love of their children (as in divorces that force children to choose between parents), and even in the ability of society's resources to come to their aid.

At a second level, unforgivable injuries take away a wounded person's belief in herself, particularly in regard to whether she has any control over the circumstances of her life. They force wounded people to question their judgment, their faith, their talents, and their values.

At the third level, the wounds destroy beliefs of the most fundamental nature—beliefs about the larger forces that work together to bring about the events in people's lives. They destroy ideas of fairness, of logic and order, of predictability and goodness, of God and man. Such essential beliefs—those about oneself and one's own attractiveness or judgment, coupled with beliefs about the world and other people in it—must be rebuilt when destroyed.

An unforgivable wound can spiral outward so that people question their beliefs about larger systems: the medical profession, for example; or law enforcement's ability to protect them; or the very concept of justice. The forgiving process is one in which both morality and meaning are defined and redefined until the world again makes sense. Until an injured person recognizes the extent of her ruptured beliefs and their essential nature, she cannot forgive. A wound cannot be forgiven unless the wounded person understands the injury's dimensions and depth and the beliefs that have fallen to it.

Private Wounds

Because unforgivable injuries begin with a transgression of a moral rule unique to the injured and injurer, it only stands to reason that the wounds are relative and private, sometimes almost too private to reveal. Telling someone about them exposes a person's most vulnerable traits and qualities.

For example, suppose an older woman, Mrs. Youngman, confides in a friend that she has thrown her adult son out of the house because he has stolen her savings. She finds she cannot forgive him. When the friend asks if he has ever done anything like that before, Mrs. Youngman is embarrassed to admit that her son has stolen many things from her over the years but that she has chosen to overlook his behavior. In the privacy of their moral agreements, she and the son have tacitly allowed stealing to be acceptable. The mother secretly blames herself for letting her son go so far and fears that she has failed both him and herself.

Like Mrs. Youngman, all people who define a wound as "unforgivable" to a friend or counselor actually expose the ways they define personal morality. They let others see the very core of their definitions of right and wrong; and they also allow them to know how far they have stretched the limits of their moral rules in order to preserve their relationships. Revealing the unforgivable exposes the forgivable.

Ann Roland's injury, like all unforgivable injuries, began with the betrayal of an agreement. Betrayed agreements can be, and usually are, forged with specific people—in the case of unforgivable injuries, intimates.

Extreme emotions are the companions of intimate betrayals. Fury tainted with grief follows an unforgivable injury of any kind, no matter what event causes it. To be betrayed by a stranger is one thing. To be morally wounded by one you have loved is quite another.

Unforgivable injuries fly straight into one's heart, into private spaces where hopes and aspirations dwell. They bring about a kind of finality—the end of a myth about one's partner (parent, friend, or child) or perhaps to dreams of a long-anticipated future (or an idealized past). When unforgivable injuries are fully experienced, their victims will never be the same.

Forgiveness is a rebirth of hope, a reorganization of thought, and a reconstruction of dreams. Once forgiving begins, dreams can be rebuilt. When forgiving is complete, meaning has been extracted from the worst of experiences and used to create a new set of moral rules and a new interpretation of life's events.

CHAPTER 2

Harms and Harmers

There are open wounds, shrunk sometimes to the size of a pin prick, but wounds still.

F. SCOTT FITZGERALD, *Tender Is the Night*

Eileen Rhodes sat peacefully on her front-porch swing on a warm Sunday afternoon. She was thirteen, and it was a sweet May in the Midwest. The Rhodeses children had returned from church, eaten Sunday dinner with their parents, and gone outdoors, as they did most spring Sundays. The smell of the fried chicken still drifted from the kitchen window and blended into the grainy scent of the alfalfa field.

Eileen was surprised when Tom, the county sheriff, drove into the farmyard. She was also surprised to see her mother and father come out onto the front porch, a suitcase in her father's hand. Quickly, her father passed the suitcase to Tom and told Eileen to go with him. She did not protest; her temper had gotten her into trouble before.

When the sheriff's car came to a stop after what seemed a lengthy ride, the girl peered out the window to see her new home: the county hospital. Eileen would live there for over thirty years, never to see the Rhodes farm or any member of her family again. Abandonment had begun a nearly lifelong unforgivable injury.

Abandonment is just one of the categories of unforgivable injuries. Altogether there are six separate categories into which these injuries can be placed: abuse (both physical and emotional); abandonment; infidelity; loss of money, job, or reputation; loss of health or life; and loss of freedom, such as forced abortion or hospitalization. Of all the kinds of people who can hurt each other, a special few cause unforgivable harm. We will call these injuries the harms of lovers and spouses, the harms of mothers and fathers, the harms of friends and co-workers, and the harms of children. Each kind of harm injures with horrible force, and each destroys different beliefs.

The Harms of Lovers and Spouses

Spouses (along with parents) are among the most potent and significant influences in the course of your life. When you make a commitment to another person, you are sending several signals, at least implicitly, to the other person, to family members, and to the community at large. First, a commitment between spouses signals that each is willing to be influenced by the other and that compromises between them will alter each one's life. In a sense, when you marry, it is an open acknowledgment that you have made a choice that will require you to negotiate and alter some of your own objectives in life. People may have no say about who their parents are, but they choose spouses. So when your life partner betrays you, you are damaged by a person you have chosen as one of the most powerful influences in your life. Unforgivable injuries caused by parents evoke pain and sorrow, but those brought about by spouses in all likelihood evoke pain and sorrow coupled with rage and humiliation. After all, in marriage betrayals, one has chosen one's own injurer.

Marriages break up for any number of reasons. In studies of marital dissolution, for example, women and men report very different reasons for ending relationships. Women list physical and verbal abuse, financial problems, lack of love, and drinking problems as the most common reasons. Men, by contrast, rank in-law troubles and sexual incompatibility as more common.[1] The difference between ordinary reasons for marital breakups (no matter how painful they may be) and unforgivable events that precipitate a rupture is that most of the common reasons do not involve moral breaches. People may drift away from each other, become insensitive, fall out of love, or develop different sexual appetites or desires, none of which breaches a moral contract. They just happen. Infidelity, on the other hand, is for many people the most significant violation of an agreement of trust that can ever affect them. Abuse that crosses over an agreed-upon line is another. Either of them becomes unforgivable when the moral contract between partners has forbidden it.

People whose partners were unfaithful described their injuries in many different ways, but the words of the wife of a schoolteacher express the turmoil that infidelity can cause:

> *Unlike most affairs I have ever read about, my husband managed several unique affairs with his high school students. These highly emotional and mentally intimate relationships went unobserved by everyone but me. Watching him in action destroyed me. I felt like I was the crazy one because it simply was not observable by anyone but those involved. He was an absolute* MASTER *at deceit and manipulation.*

To find evidence that one's spouse is having an affair may be the most awful pain an adult can experience. It is so hurtful not only because public promises are broken and private moral arrangements betrayed but also because all sorts of other betrayals are revealed as a result. Unfaithful partners have usually lied or withheld information; they have often feigned emotional involvement or sexual excitement where there was little left; and many have even drained some of the couple's finances if an affair has gone on for a long time.

Infidelity, once uncovered, swiftly destroys other beliefs. For many people, the rapid losses are so sudden that the already injured fall prey to even more pain. Many people become physically sick or barely able to function at work. Some even lose the will to live. They conclude that if this person has betrayed them, the world has betrayed them, too. To those individuals whose life's meaning is wrapped up in their marriage, infidelity can deal a nearly fatal blow.

Ned's experience shows how nearly fatal infidelity can be:

I got so obsessed with the situation I could barely function. Most days I'd just drag into work and accomplish nothing. I felt like everyone knew—like they could see through me and they pitied me. I got confused and forgot to pay bills. I screwed up a huge project I'd been working on and lost a contract. I thought about running my wife and her lover over with my car and killing both of them. At three o'clock in the morning, I'd be sitting in the dark so full of hate I wasn't sure if I got a gun who I'd kill.

Then I thought, You'd better watch it; you've lost enough. For God's sake, don't lose whatever is left.

Infidelity is profoundly painful for another reason. If a spouse dies, the loss is accompanied by deep grief; the grief, though, does not stem from the partner's decision to leave his widowed spouse. But if a spouse chooses to be unfaithful, the infidelity not only robs the betrayed of companionship and love (if divorce follows and sometimes even if it does not); it also robs the betrayed of the future he had anticipated while his betrayer's future unfolds right before his eyes. The end of a dream, one of life's most painful endings, is not allowed to play itself out in fantasy, as it often does when a spouse dies. Instead, every day, the dreams one had for the future are assaulted by the reality of the betrayer's continued existence. Every day is a confrontation with what will never be—perhaps security, safety, comfort, financial stability, total trust in another person, predictability, or the companionship of someone to share parenthood or the dream of becoming grandparents together. Infidelity shatters dreams. And since this particular dream has been shattered, whether or not the marriage continues, it will never be the same. The love of a marriage is changed as a result of the unforgivable breach.

Abuse also shatters a dream, this one likely to be the hope that violent behavior will cease or that the marriage will improve over time. Abuse that crosses over an acceptable line ends other beliefs as surely as infidelity does. Harriet, who tried hard to keep her abusive marriage together, put it this way:

> *When I finally left him, I lost some of my self-respect. My mother had lived with my father for years, and he had abused her, especially when he drank. She took her vows seriously, though. You know, "in sickness and in health." If alcoholism is a sickness, she knew she had to stay with him, even when he was hurting her. So she stuck to her vows, but I couldn't. I just wish I'd been as strong as my mother was.*

Three major forms of dreams die when spouses wound each other: the dream that one is in command of the world and that all is predictable and well; the dream that another person is the personification of all that is good—someone who can be depended on to be there no matter what else transpires; or the dream that if one person behaves consistently and predictably, so will other people, particularly one's spouse. When the first dream is assaulted, the betrayed person experiences what I have called the Pilot-in-Command Injury. When a spouse experiences the second kind of wound, he has suffered the Defenseless-Drifter Injury. The third kind of injury is the Mathematician's Injury.

THE PILOT-IN-COMMAND INJURY

Pilot in Command is a concept used in aviation. The pilot is responsible for the safety of his aircraft and for making decisions in the cockpit. If the aircraft has a beautiful trip capped off by a picture-perfect landing, the pilot takes credit. He also assumes responsibility for any bad judgment. The nature of the flight rests on his skills.

Alongside the Pilot in Command, there are those who are not in charge. They may navigate, make suggestions, offer opinions, and even fly part of the way, but they are subordinate. To the Pilot in Command, the world is his to have. The airplane does what he makes it do.

To people like Pilots in Command, an unforgivable injury begins with an unexpected jolt to their sense of mastery or control over the environment and everything in it. This jolt usually comes from a trusted subordinate. The following parable illustrates the point:

> *Crisp, a crusty old pilot, has been accompanied by Smith, the silent navigator, for ten years now. Crisp commands; Crisp flies; Crisp gets credit. Smith reads the weather map, plots the chart, prechecks the engine, and communicates with the tower.*
>
> *One day, Crisp looks over at Smith and sees that he has a parachute on. He says, "Smith, why the parachute?" Smith replies, "I'm jumping. See if you can fly this thing or find an increase in salary for me." Crisp, true to form, looks steadily forward and says, "I fly this airplane." In answer, Smith opens the door and jumps. Crisp is astonished; then he is angry. Then he realizes he doesn't know where he is. He gets a little dizzy. He begins to call the tower but doesn't know how. He sees a weather front up ahead but doesn't know where the edges are. As he flies into a great bank of cumulus clouds, the plane lurches sideways, the result of Crisp's total fear and now his vertigo. He launches into a dive straight at the ground. As he heads toward the ground below, through the whirling clouds he sees Smith just ahead, quietly floating in his parachute. As Crisp's diving plane comes abreast of Smith, Crisp, with his last bit of energy and with fear-parched throat, forces the window open and yells out into the sky, "Damn you, Smith. I'm the Pilot in Comand here, not you."*

A Pilot in Command believes that his marriage is fully in his control and that his partner is stable, predictable, and subordinately supportive. When an unfaithful spouse takes the unanticipated action of having an affair or betraying the moral rules in some other way, the Pilot-in-Command type falls apart—not because his "helpmate" has been lost but because he is forced to recognize how helpless and fragile he really is. This time, the pilot is not the one calling all the shots; someone else is.

The description by thirty-three-year-old Janet of her marriage illustrates how these injuries may proceed from a marital betrayal:

> *We had an agreement that if he ever had an affair, he had twenty-four hours to get out of town. Then it was open season. But this was no joke. It just knocked me down. First I was nauseated, then angry; and then I felt helpless, devastated, and exposed. My ego was crushed. I felt helpless because I didn't know what to do about the conditions that led to his infidelity.*
>
> *The helplessness I felt was just impossible. I had no options. The only option I could come up with was murder. I told him he had to stop or else. It was really more like a man would respond, I guess. I could not tolerate this. Then he said he would stop, but he didn't. And that was real helplessness.*
>
> *My vulnerability was the biggest harm. See, I am a very controlled person. To be that vulnerable was very scary. I didn't know I was* THAT *vulnerable to* THAT *individual.*
>
> *The infidelity was the finale, but it wasn't the hardest, most important part of the incident. What led up to it was harder to deal with. It was like the end of an ideal, like a coming down to earth. It's like—he's human. I had to give up the imagined person I thought I was marrying. So the choices were to reconcile with the real person or divorce and find some other person who was another fantasy and start all over.*

Judy, who had been used to getting her own way in relationships, described her Pilot-in-Command Injury like this:

> *I had been going with this guy for three and a half years; we had an argument one night, and I broke off the relationship. I always broke off the relationship, and he'd go home and he'd call. Well, a few days later, I reconsidered the whole thing. I mean,*

I really did love him. But when I tried to call him, he was with
another woman. I couldn't believe it. This thing got me down
like nothing else ever had. I got depressed, and I lost weight, got
real sick. I mean, I've been spoiled before—I'm a really selfish
person. But this brought me to my knees.

For a betrayed spouse to realize that presumed control over his
world can come undone as a result of a partner's actions is terrifying.
The wounded person not only faces the loss of trust in his partner
and the moral transgressions that accompany an unforgivable injury
but also the loss of a probably well established assumption that he
is in charge of life itself. A Pilot in Command betrayed by infidelity
will, like all injured people, attempt to regain control; but when he
realizes he cannot control his partner, he also realizes that he is out
of control and so is his world. The result is terror filled with fury.
In this kind of injury, the first beliefs to fall are those the injured
person has about himself. Then he realizes that the way he has
perceived his spouse is inaccurate. Finally, control over other
things—children; in-laws, perhaps; the timing of events; or the terms
of contracts—becomes totally nonexistent. He spirals from loss of
beliefs about himself to those about significant others to those about
less significant others until the whole world crumbles into a confused
heap. It is from this position that he must start the forgiving process.

THE DEFENSELESS-DRIFTER INJURY

Unlike the take-charge Pilot in Command, others believe that they
are not in charge of much at all. They drift through life hoping to
find people who will protect them from pain. They feel defenseless
and unable to protect themselves or to find their own purpose in
life. Others' goals become their own. In essence, they are searching
for someone who loves unconditionally and will see to it that they
are protected from the world's onslaughts. Defenseless Drifters often
view the world as an unsafe, hostile place and hope some protector
will stand between them and all that is threatening.

In some small way, each of us looks for a protector; yet most of us also learn to protect ourselves and even other people. But to those people whose tightly woven moral agreements with their spouses implicitly or explicitly state that the other will never do harm and, conversely, that the more vulnerable party is inviolably safe, the injury caused by an unfaithful spouse is almost unutterably painful. If a partner is unfaithful or crosses the boundary of tolerated abuse, the defender-protector who kept the beast of harm from the door becomes that beast. The protector harms. Lost is the myth of safety, and the belief comes tumbling down.

Cheryl, a psychotherapist in her early thirties, described the shattering of her belief that her husband would protect her unconditionally:

> *I always felt vulnerable. I was from an abusive family—I saw that love hurt. So trust wasn't there. I was fat, and if you're fat, friends taunted you. So trust meant unconditional acceptance. I needed him to be all of those things. I trusted that he was. I think when I found out about his affair I thought, My God, he's human, too. It touched into all those other things where I'd been disappointed. [She begins to cry.] Oh, God, this is embarrassing. My clients think I'm so sensitive. They don't know I can't help but cry. So it works out well that way.*

Like so many others who suffered a Defenseless-Drifter Injury because of their partner's infidelity, the recollection of the injury brought tears to this school guidance counselor's eyes even though several years had passed since the hurt and her marriage was still intact:

> *We were always a couple, intensely such a couple, to the exclusion of dating others. And for two years, I thought, This is like heaven; this is what life is all about. Life was intense and wonderful, and I was very happy. But in restrospect, I didn't really see him as a person. I had him on a pedestal. He was a big man on campus. And I know that was unhealthy. He came off the pedestal the first time I saw him with another woman. Initially, you see,*

I was very emotionally dependent. I mean, the fear of not having him and having to grow up too quickly was more fear inducing than having to come to grips with this.

People who suffer a Defenseless-Drifter Injury because of abuse rather than infidelity experience a different pain. Diana describes it this way:

Usually after he'd beat me, he was really sorry and would buy me something. I think he told himself he wouldn't do it again; he'd always been drinking. This time, though, after he pulled the knife, he seemed resigned that it would happen again. It was my second marriage, and I needed him and needed it to work. But I had to accept it. I'd always said the abuse would stop, but after the knife attack, I had to walk away.

It is a painful situation for a person to depend on a protector who is at the same time a harmer. If you reject the harmer, you lose the protector. This, though, is the position the Defenseless Drifter finds himself in before he can begin to forgive.

THE MATHEMATICIAN'S INJURY

For some people, moral rules in relationships become ends in themselves instead of a means of negotiating right and wrong. When this happens, people begin to see the world through sets of equations. They begin to believe that if one partner behaves in a predictable way, the other will respond predictably. If one tells the truth, so will the other; if one keeps promises, so will the other. A Mathematician does not consider that another might change the rules on his side of the relationship's equation unless, or until, he has done the same. Unpredictability does not fit into a Mathematician's orderly construct of the way the world operates. So when something unpredictable happens, Mathematicians are devastated. Rules, rather than subordinates or assurances that one will be protected, have made the world a safe place in which to live.

Dan, a policeman, described the crumbling of his predictable world.

> *I had been married for twenty-one years. I knew almost right away that I'd made a mistake, but I thought marriage was forever. (I'd been raised a Presbyterian, and that's what I'd been taught.) I had three boys and stayed married for them. So when I got into financial trouble, of course I expected her to be loyal. But she betrayed me. She wouldn't go back to work or try to borrow from her parents after everything I'd done. Things began to fall apart. She would not change. It all led to divorce, but I'm still aware that I didn't do what I set out to do. I mean I didn't stay married forever.*

Of course, personality types like the Pilot in Command, the Defenseless Drifter, or the Mathematician are not cast in concrete. People may combine the characteristics of all three. A person may be dependent but controlling, for example. Most people form assumptions about their most intimate relationships. It is your assumptions about the people closest to you that make one of these types more descriptive of you than the other two. Knowing which type most closely fits your assumptions will help you understand your injury better.

The pain in finding that one is not in control of the goings-on in one's life, that one's husband or wife will no longer be around to count on unconditionally, or that rules do not work is excruciating. Much is lost in each kind of injury. Lost is the belief that certain truths have underpinned the marriage. Lost is part of the past that infidelity, for example, reveals was cloaked in deceit and disloyalty. A betrayal of marriage can unveil a secret history that has been unfolding without the wounded person's knowledge. A spouse betrayed by an affair must even lose a sense of validity in his own history. Looking back on what was supposedly real, a person betrayed by unfaithfulness is faced squarely with more questions than answers: "When did this begin? Did he ever really love me? Was that a lie he told me that weekend? Is that why the money has been low?" History is filled with questions. The validity of one's own experience is thrown over to suspicion, fury, and grief.

Gone, too, is the wounded spouse's vision of his future. If the past and present were lies, so, too, must be the anticipated future.

Infidelity or abuse can break people's hearts. A betraying spouse has shared in cocreating the fabric of another person's life. Infidelity or unacceptable violence reveals all too painfully that at least part of one's life's fabric was woven from the lies of a dissembling weaver.

The Harms of Mothers and Fathers

Mothers and fathers, like husbands and wives, shape our lives and make us who we are. Husbands and wives shape the adult in us. Mothers and fathers shape the child in us and, in part, the adult who evolves from that child. Like spouses, parents can abuse, abandon, force behavioral compliance, and betray promises; but unlike spouses, parents who unforgivably betray children do not assault well-formed belief systems. Instead, they assault beliefs in the process of being formulated and stabilized. They assault ideas in the making and values that have not yet taken hold.

To use an analogy, when a parent unforgivably wounds his child, it is as if he walks through the child's play area and without reason kicks down a stack of building blocks the youngster has lovingly and tediously constructed. Since most unforgivable wounds by parents are results of continuing behaviors and not onetime events, the analogy might be more accurate if the parent were to randomly and repeatedly destroy the child's stack of building blocks for no particular reason. A child to whom this happens would learn several important lessons: First, he would learn that he cannot create without fear of having his creation destroyed. Second, he would learn that he cannot anticipate the results of his labor; something that once had form and structure can swiftly become a strewn-about and incomprehensible collection of disconnected pieces. He would learn that even if the stack were rebuilt, the blocks would not be put back just as they were, but in slightly different shape and order. And he would finally accept that no matter what he does, his work would sooner or later be toppled over and once again have to be created from scratch.

Once beliefs have been damaged repeatedly, children may simply wander through their young lives trying on and testing one set of personal standards after another to see what, if anything, fits. Some people injured in childhood take years to construct a firm notion of right and wrong and an idea that there are moral rules between people.

Carla, a thirty-six-year-old successful political writer, described her parents' abuse of her this way.

> *I had a very traumatic experience caused by my father, and it took me nearly twenty years to finally be able to say, "I forgive you," and* MEAN *it.*
>
> *When I was fifteen, Dad married an alcoholic, my mother having died the year before. Dad's wife hated me so much that she literally threw me out of the house, refusing to live there if I remained. Instead of Dad seeking family counseling or some alternative, he simply told me he knew I could take care of myself and aided my stepmother in evicting me from "home" while I was in the tenth grade.*
>
> *Needless to say, I was hurt badly by Dad's obvious lack of concern for me, and the emotional damage caused by him created a multitude of problems over the years, especially in my relationships with my husbands and children.*
>
> *Finally, after locating a good therapist and getting help from him, I was able to recognize and voice my hostility toward my father and discuss what had happened, and, in time, I then forgave him.*

Other people I talked to were raped by fathers and grandfathers. One woman's mother had made her eat off the floor and tied her to a piano leg for hours on end. Sylvia's parents abused her severely and repeatedly. For some reason, though, one particular incident broke her spirit and destroyed her shaky belief in herself and in her parents' stability and kindheartedness.

> *I am a 52-year-old married woman. I was born to a very mean, cruel, sadistic, raving maniac of a father. My mother was a very dull, passive, no-personality person. My first memories outside of hunger were at about seven years of age, when I was learning to write. I was very proud. I got my paper and pencil. I was going to show my parents how I could write. My father held me down and made me write over and over again, "Sylvia is a fool." From that moment, I was never the same.*

Sylvia spent hundreds of hours in therapy and untold pain as she tried to sort through the extent of her wounds.

For obvious reasons, and some not so obvious, unforgivable injuries to children are slightly different from adult-to-adult injuries. While all unforgivable injuries assault beliefs and violate moral contracts, the wounds that adults inflict on one another are sudden blows to established assumptions. Wounds to children, on the other hand, happen before assumptions are translated into beliefs and sometimes even before the rules defining acceptable and unacceptable treatment among people who supposedly love each other have been well established. This is the tricky aspect of unforgivable injuries to children. Although we have said that unforgivable injuries begin with an unforgivable event that violates a shared definition of right and wrong, people who are wounded as children may not recognize their wounds as such for many years. This is because an adult can negotiate a moral agreement with another adult and set limits to acceptable behaviors. An adult knows when those limits have been breached. When very young children are concerned, though, only adults, most of whom are the child's parents, define what is right or wrong. Parents define "right" and "wrong" through their words and actions, and until a child grows up a little, he simply accepts his parents' definitions.[2] For this reason, if a child is raised in a home where hitting is morally acceptable, then hitting is not unforgivable. If verbal attacks are normal, they, too, are not unforgivable.

ABUSE AND PUNISHMENT

Most childhood victims of unforgivable injuries are either physically or emotionally abused or both. Abuse involving children is a complicated matter. Although most adults can discern what is abuse and what is not, very young children may not be able to distinguish punishment from outright undeserved abuse. Both punishment and abuse can come in the same form. Spanking, verbal reproaches, slapping, or locking one away in a room can all be forms of abuse or forms of punishment. Because of this, a young child can be easily confused as to which is which. But punishment differs from abuse in several vital ways.

Both punishment and abuse make one person the object of another person's will. A punished or abused person is required to defer to another's will and to lose (temporarily at least) his personal power and control over events that are taking place. But punishment has three other critical components that distinguish it from abuse. Punishment follows the breaking of a specific rule. In abuse, no specific rule needs to have been broken. Punishment is weighted to be approximately equivalent to the rule that was broken. It is fair. Abuse is not equivalent to any infraction. If a person's parking meter runs over a few minutes, he may be required to pay a ten-dollar ticket. That is his punishment: He is the subject of the will of the city council. If he were required to pay $500 for his meter's running over a few minutes, one could judge that the city council was abusing its citizenry; the punishment is disproportionate to the "crime." It is the same situation if a child were made to eat excrement (as one woman I talked with was forced to do) because he was a few minutes late from school. A rule was broken, but the punishment is out of proportion to the tardiness. Abuse is not equal in weight to any broken rule. Punishment serves to teach and clean the slate; abuse serves to hurt.

Carla, whose father and stepmother threw her out of the house, related more about her abuse:

> *I managed to lie about my age and find a little apartment when I was about sixteen. But they knew where I was and would come get me whenever they wanted something. Like, when my stepmother had relatives come from out of town, they would come get me and dress me up—like an organ grinder's monkey or something. I'd entertain, and when it was over, they'd boot me back out. But I still tried to please them.*

A problem with the harms of mothers and fathers is that children who are abused might think they are being punished. Even worse, they sometimes grow to think that the abuse they suffer serves to repair their relationship with the parent.[3] After all, punishment allows people to start afresh. So young children who cannot distinguish punishment from abuse may come to believe that abuse will allow them to start a relationship afresh also.

When a child is hurt by a parent, the child often believes he deserves it. He also thinks he has breached his relationship with the parent and must somehow mend it.[4] The repair is accomplished through atonement or by restoring harmony. Pain itself signals to some children that the rupture between his parents and himself has been mended and that the relationship between them has been reestablished. Thus, to some children, abuse equals punishment equals atonement equals repairing a relationship. Such beliefs can last a long time, until the wounded person recognizes that abuse did not equal punishment. It was abuse and nothing more.

Carla finally sought help from her school guidance counselor. When she left his office, the counselor immediately called her father and stepmother, who later that evening beat her mercilessly. Still, Carla tried to please both of them, hoping that they would finally take her back in. She thought the beating might end her exile and restore her father's love for her.

The infliction of injuries by mothers and fathers affect their children's beliefs in a number of other ways. First, the adults who have been injured as children might see the world as a place where injuries go on all the time. They might view themselves as people who are dominated by the will of others and who have little choice as to what goes on in their lives. They might think that physical aggression mends ruptured relationships. They might believe that they deserve to be hurt. They might think that everyone is abusive or that rules make no sense.

Maria, who was sexually assaulted and abandoned by her father when she was eight, felt this way.

> *I felt illegitimate—like a misfit. I was afraid to sit by myself. It seemed like I was always afraid of being left or of being alone. That feeling went on for a long time and sometimes still comes up. I never know what to expect.*

Carla and Maria and others who are hurt during childhood may eventually come to label their injuries unforgivable, *but only when they discover that it was their parents who breached moral obligations to them, not the other way around.*

The unforgivable harms of mothers and fathers run deep, sometimes so deep that they go unrecognized. They are like knives driven into an apple just as it is forming. Even as the sweet flesh grows around the core, the wound becomes an integral part of the fruit. Unlike the swift, shattering wounds of spouses and lovers, the wounds of parents are insidious, thwarting a child's attempts to forgive because the moral development of the adult takes time to overtake the experiences of the child. When an adult can finally say, "That was wrong, and I was not fairly treated," he can recognize the unforgivable injury at last, confront it, and begin to find its edges and the extent of the damage done.

The abuse suffered by children, like the wounds of spouses, alters a sufferer permanently. Belief after belief is sullied because of the unforgivable injury.

Randy, whose mother's affair and subsequent remarriage resulted in his hatred of her for many years, lost several significant beliefs,

the most important one being that it is good to talk to people about
feelings.

> *I learned that you can't really talk to anyone else. Who wants
> to be burdened with your feelings? So I held everything in. I
> think I was carrying my father's grief around. Then it all came
> undone. I went on a three-week drunk. I quit my job. The work
> didn't seem to make sense to me. I started to gamble a lot; and
> finally, I broke. At the time, I had developed ulcers, and I'd just
> sit and bawl.*

Children are more likely to see the world as a place where they
cannot be Pilots in Command and where no one is trustworthy.
Once harmed, many decide that what little control they have centers
on their own accomplishments. These they can at least gain some
mastery over. If a person is too young to control his life and too
distrustful to let someone protect him, a child can, at least for a
while, create a safe little world for himself. One day, as an adult, he
will come face-to-face with his wounds and with the need to forgive
something that happened many years before.

The Harms of Friends and Co-workers

Friends and co-workers are also capable of causing unforgivable
injuries. While they may be less common than the harms of parents
and spouses, those of friends, too, can cause great pain.

Friendships, like other intimate relationships, are sustained
through a presumed implicit trust. In strong friendships as in marriages, people extend their hearts and possessions to each other, share
each other's secrets, and trust that no one will use the friendship for
his own advantage or do intentional harm to the other. The harms
of friends can be wide ranging, from a seemingly minor offense like
being late to dinner to the injury of reputations and even future
financial security. Here is the story of Martha, a teacher, whose life
would never be the same because of her best friend.

> *I had put five years of teacher retirement money into investment-grade diamonds. To save sales tax, I had mailed them to another state to a friend. She kept the diamonds in her bank for a year. Then I called and asked to have them sent to me. On her way to the post office (where she would have insured them), she went to a Kmart to shop. She left her purse on a counter accidentally. When she realized she had no purse, she ran to that counter, and it was gone. So was my $14,000 worth of diamonds. They were never found. Since they were not insured, I lost everything.*

As this account indicates, people do not necessarily call something unforgivable only if they decide the unforgivable event was intentional. An unintentional act can result in unforgivable harm just as an intentional one can. Perceived intentionality is not at the core of what makes something unforgivable. What does is that fundamental beliefs are shattered. Martha lost her fantasy of a down payment on a home. After all her years of hard work and saving, she had no control over her financial future. Her friend's unintentional but careless act had altered her life plan permanently.

There are other ways that friends and co-workers wound each other, less dramatic, perhaps, than losing diamonds but potentially as far reaching. Friends who are also co-workers can deal tremendous blows. Many people who work in offices or businesses experience this situation: Two people become close friends early in their career; but since no two people progress at the same rate, one is promoted before the other, or one gets a larger bonus or raise than the other. The friendship to this point is not betrayed, although competition, jealousy, and envy may have sullied it. But if one person does something self-promoting at the other's expense (e.g., if one claims the other's work as his own or withholds information about the other's significant contributions to a joint project), the friendship is breached. This often happens when two friends are rivals for a promotion. The betrayed person feels he can no longer trust friends at work and finds it hard to forgive other co-workers who might have known about the betrayer's duplicity.

Jeanette and her husband started a business with a very good friend and her husband. Jeanette became their confidante, member of the same card club, and the foursome's mediator and troubleshooter. Suddenly, the other couple announced that they were leaving the business to start their own. They gave Jeanette and her husband less than a week to decide whether or not to buy them out. Jeanette described the breach this way:

> *This was the hardest thing that ever happened to me. I considered the other couple about our closest friends. After they pulled out, many of our friends gave us the impression that they liked the other couple, so we felt like oddballs. We had the feeling that our former friends preferred them to us and would not associate with us if the other couple was present. Then my brother-in-law realized his new job was not panning out, so he joined our former partners in business! It was such a blow to us.*

Friends can also harm each other through engaging in petty gossip. Joe, a businessman in his thirties, tells how gossip threatened his business and his marriage.

> *I am thirty-three years old and have been separated from my wife of almost twelve years for the past two and one-half months. For the past year and a half my wife has carried a diagnosis of terminal cancer that has caused several operations, a series of radiation treatments, and a broad array of chemotherapy treatments. Her current chemo treatments appear to be effective in reducing the cancer and hence, for a change, greatly improve her prognosis.*
>
> *The cause for our separation was, in fact, the involvement, by several people who work for me and with me, in spreading rumors and stories concerning my personal conduct and behavior. When the information that was being transmitted through the grapevine was made known to my wife by some "friends" that we knew jointly—people who still work for me—my wife requested that I leave.*

The businessman had to reassess his friendships and decide whether to fire all his workers or retain them so that his business could continue to run smoothly. His predicament was not unlike that of a person living in a house with a spouse who has betrayed him. The businessman or betrayed spouse can hang on to rage or forgive and attempt to salvage either the marriage or the business. Whichever the decision, the nature of relationships will have permanently changed because beliefs about people have changed as a result of the wound.

Friendships—and less so, relationships with co-workers—are among the most important kinds of relationships in most people's lives. Apart from family members, most of us spend what remains of our personal time with our friends. For some people, friends take the place of family; and for many women at least, best friends are almost as essential as spouses, particularly when it comes to sharing feelings. As one woman said when she found out her best friend was having an affair with her husband:

> She broke my heart. I loved her so much and for so long, I went home and got sick when I found out. It was as if she had torn my heart out.

We have special relationships and special sets of expectations with our friends. Because with friends there aren't the financial entanglements or the extended-family relationships that we enjoy with spouses, friendships may be purer than marital relationships. Like spouses, friends are people we choose. The choice may not signal to the public or family members that a friend will have influence over life decisions we make.

But enduring friends are essential in helping people to think through life decisions they may make and to get back on course when confusion or conflict are affecting one's life. The moral history between good friends may include being honest, providing mutual support, retaining secrets, and, above all, not harming. When friends hurt each other, the wounds can be deep, but not in the sense that children are wounded or in the way that a spouse's betrayal can alter the very shape of a life. Friends' wounds can damage the concept of pure trust itself. A friend's unforgivable lie can signal that nowhere is there anyone who simply can be trusted for trust's sake. The loss of the belief in trust itself is like the loss of beliefs suffered in other unforgivable injuries. It goes to the core of a person and how he thereafter views his world. Unforgivable injuries of friends and co-workers can wound as deeply as those of spouses and children. Only the belief that is damaged is a different belief. Nonetheless, the wound of a friend, a wound to trust itself, can forever alter a person's concept of people, self, and the world.

The Harms of Children

Children can wound their parents in an exceptional variety of ways. It may be, however, that even if children have many methods of dealing blows to parents, few of the blows are perceived by parents as unforgivable. Most people I talked with readily forgave their children even if they forgave others with difficulty.

Moral contracts between parents and children ordinarily allow for boundaries that can be stretched, by the children at least, beyond the limits of other kinds of relationships. Children can steal, fail, lie, lose money, ruin their marriages, or drain their parents' resources dry and still be accepted. While parents may not approve of their children's behavior or condone their misdeeds, few people I talked with saw their children as provoking unforgivable breaches. The exceptions are these: when children cut off communication with their parents without any apparent reason or when they refuse to heed a parent's warnings and then get into trouble. Both signal perceived disloyalty.

At the heart of many moral contracts between parents and their children is a central rule: The child is free to fail or thrive, but he must not be disloyal. A sudden disloyal event can evolve into a full unforgivable injury. Beatrice describes her daughter's unforgivable disloyalty:

The last time I ever saw my daughter, she had called me an asshole. I couldn't believe she'd stoop so low. She was angry at me because I wanted to fly back home to the States early. But to do that? Before I left, I tried to reconcile. Her friends even came over and tried to help, but it didn't work. She just got angry and said she wanted nothing more to do with me. I could forgive her name-calling, but I couldn't forgive that. I haven't seen her for over two years now.

When a parent is damaged by his child, the following questions arise: "What was all of my sacrifice worth?" and "How did I fail?" If the breach severs their relationship permanently, a parent is cut off not from his future as a maturing adult (as happens when a marriage fails) but from the rejuvenation and youthfulness that children bring into one's life—an awful loss.

Summary

The harms of unforgivable injurers go to the heart of a person's beliefs. People who hurt their spouses challenge their victims' assumptions about what control a person really has over his destiny or how much trust and faith one can put in another's ability to guide his life. Children harmed by parents may come to rely solely on themselves for their survival or well-being. Once unforgivably wounded by a parent, a child may never again see people as sources of safety or intimacy as a protective net. People harmed by friends or co-workers may lose their faith in their judgment or their profession. People hurt by their children lose the presumption that their mature years will be happy and uncontaminated.

By definition, unforgivable injuries destroy beliefs about oneself, other people, and the world in general. Depending on which kind of harmer causes such a devastating wound, one of the levels of beliefs is probably more shattered than the other two. Still, all three are permanently altered.

The harms of lovers and spouses, mothers and fathers, children, and friends and acquaintances are the most deadly harms of all. They *are* the unforgivable. They can break people's spirits or finally be overcome. Whichever, an unforgivably wounded person is changed; but changes need not be for the worse if people can conquer them through forgiving.

CHAPTER **3**

The Aftermath of Injury

And now a bubble burst, and now a world.
ALEXANDER POPE

Randy Simpson rode his bicycle home from school along the familiar streets between his grade school and his house. It was midmorning, and he was riding home with a note from the school nurse. His nose had started to bleed in gym class, and when the nurse could not reach Mrs. Simpson by phone, she decided to send Randy home to rest.

Randy pulled his bicycle into the backyard and entered the house through the back door. For some reason, he did not call out to his mother as he normally did, but instead went down the hallway toward his room. When he passed his parents' bedroom, he heard strange noises. He yelled out loud when he saw his mother and a strange man, both without clothes on, in his parents' bed.

Randy remembered only confusion for months afterward. He recollected telling his father about what he saw over the pleading protests of his mother. He recalled the screaming and arguing of his parents night after night. And he especially remembered the empty pit in his stomach as his mother packed her bags and finally drove away. Although blurry, he recalled testifying in court as his mother sat drooped over and weeping. Later and thereafter, he remembered, more than anything else, her dark, bitter eyes piercing him with hatred whenever she saw him.

Randy's mother went on to marry the "strange" man. Randy went on to blame himself, hate his mother, get into trouble, cut off all relationships with his mother's family, and pity his father. He sealed himself in a cocoon of hatred from which he did not emerge for some fifteen years.

In *Life After Marriage*,[1] Alfred Alvarez describes the effects of divorce on a woman he knew:

> *She had suffered a mutilation and was in shock, like the victim of a terrorist outrage: part of herself had been blown away and nothing was going to sew it back on again.*

In the immediate wake of any unforgivable injury, enormous emotional upheaval takes place. I call this time of upheaval the *aftermath period*.

The aftermath period is as filled with futility as the terrorist victim's attempts to sew on a severed limb; and it can be just as painful. It is characterized by shock, confusion, disbelief, rage, helplessness, and a kind of terrible impotence. In addition, many wounded people experience physical illnesses or symptoms. Some suffer headaches, sleeplessness, rectal bleeding, weight loss, miscarriages, hallucinations, and gastrointestinal problems; some also drink heavily. The period can last for weeks or even months. But what is important to understand is that it is normal. The period may be upsetting for both the injured and those who comfort them; but it is entirely normal.

The aftermath period is so highly charged and emotionally complex because victims of an unforgivable event are not clear whether the injury is complete. In other words, they cannot tell whether everything that is going to happen has finally transpired. As a result, rage cannot be pure. Nor can grief. Competing emotions are heaped on one another: grief with rage; sorrow with love; and hope with a kind of desperate, final fear. The harmed are out of control, events seem almost random, and people are hostages to their own naked vulnerability. If the complexity of the aftermath of an unforgivable injury is understood, wounded people and those who try to comfort them can accept this turbulent period as one that can be shortened, perhaps, but not avoided. It is simply part of being unforgivably harmed.

Emotional Dimensions of the Aftermath Period

There are two common pitfalls that injured people and those who comfort them can stumble upon if they lack knowledge of the aftermath period or make hasty judgments. First, the injured can expect of themselves, or their friends or family members can expect them, to blame the injurer, "bite the bullet," and get on with life when doing so would be premature. As one woman whose husband left her stated:

> *Oh, my family just said, "He was always just a jerk. You're lucky it happened. Now you can get rid of him and go on with your life."*

She was hardly ready to go on. If a badly injured person moves through the aftermath too quickly, she may postpone the necessary grieving process that must accompany all losses.

Second, the injured can, for lack of knowing how to end it, allow the aftermath period to go on for too long. If the upheaval of the aftermath is protracted beyond what helping friends expect, they may turn away from the victim in exasperation. The aftermath can be protracted because the loss of beliefs associated with the unforgivable injury is so profound that the full extent of the damage is realized fully only as more time passes. Or it can become protracted because people cannot stop blaming themselves for the injury. Either is likely to happen; but self-blame in unforgivable injuries is always to be expected.

SELF-BLAME

In the aftermath period, injured people are searching for reason. "How could this have happened?" or "What could I have done to prevent this?" are the most common questions. To a loved one or friend watching a wounded person suffer the immediate shock of an unforgivable injury, self-blame doesn't seem to make sense. Why would someone pile the additional burden of self-blame onto an already damaged ego and broken heart? The wife of a man who had been engaged in homosexual relationships expressed it this way:

> *Oh, yes. I blamed myself. I said, "What if I'd been a better lover? Maybe if I hadn't weighed so much. Maybe then he wouldn't have had to do that."*

A woman whose husband walked out without warning said:

> *I thought maybe, you know, if I had gone on the trip with him or even paid more attention to his changes, he wouldn't have needed to have an affair. I couldn't bear that pain—thinking I should have done SOMETHING differently. I just didn't know what.*

A man fired from his job by his alcoholic father told me:

> *He just needed love so badly and never got any that he just continued to hurt people himself. I thought if I loved him more, I could bring out the love in him.*

Self-blame seems to be self-defeating and unnecessarily harsh. There is, however, an important, almost universal reason for this aftermath reaction, where extraordinarily painful injuries are concerned. Self-blame allows a wounded person to make at least *some* sense out of a world turned upside down. It allows people to find some order in their shaken-up world. Even people injured by total strangers will react by blaming themselves.[2]

Self-blame gives people hope because they believe that if they can change themselves, they may be able to prevent the full loss of an unforgivable injury. Self-blame gives people hope, too, because it allows them to believe that if they have control over themselves, they can still have some control over the events of their lives. In injuries other than unforgivable offenses (e.g., deaths of children through illnesses, rapes by strangers, airplane accidents in which loved ones die, burglaries, and even wartime deaths in faraway countries), people who survive experience some degree of self-blame.[3]

A mother in her late fifties whose son was an adult living for a long time away from home still blamed herself for his death by drug overdose.

> *We said, "Why weren't we kinder to him? Why did we yell at him? Why did we criticize him so much?" Then I thought, Maybe I shouldn't have had five kids. Maybe I didn't know how to be a mother. It was all a part of the guilt package.*

Blaming herself made this woman feel that there was some reason her son died. It was not a random, meaningless happening.

Self-blame is central to the aftermath period. It should be anticipated and accepted. It serves a function and is part of an exceedingly complex set of emotions. Injured people and those who try to support them immediately after their injuries should understand this and accept it as a paradoxical, if bitter, by-product of a deep wound. It may seem self-defeating, but it really serves to help the wounded stabilize themselves so that they can later begin the forgiving process.

RAGE

Most unforgivably injured people experience not only disbelief and self-blame but absolute rage. Cheryl, the psychotherapist who discovered her husband's infidelity, began a two-day whirlwind of rage. She knew the lover and where the woman lived. She also knew where the woman's student records were kept in the university's psychology department.

> *I hated that woman's guts. I wanted to hurt her in a physical way. So—I can't believe I did this—I stole her records from the student files and found out she had aborted my husband's baby! It's hard to say this—I smashed up his pictures and drove around town like a madwoman. Then this all culminated when I got into her house and got a knife and slashed up her furniture, particularly her bed. Looking back, it's hard for me to believe I did that.*

When objects are taken from us, we, like children in a playground, rail in fury. When our beliefs are being taken from us, we are also filled with wrath. Some people express rage openly and externally; others experience it by turning it on themselves.

For the most part, people injured by spouses, friends, and other adults direct at least part of their anger outward during the aftermath. People who are hurt by parents, on the other hand, are more likely to turn it inward in the form of self-loathing. Most adults harmed by other adults seem to convert self-blame to other-blame more easily than do harmed children. In contrast to adults, children harmed by parents have a more difficult time turning their rage away from themselves toward their parents. Rage turned inward can express itself in suicide attempts. In fact, almost all of those I talked with who were abused by parents had thought about or attempted suicide. Carla, whose father and stepmother so abused her, put it this way:

> *I decided I wanted to kill myself. If I didn't do it first, I was afraid they would. They might have taken everything else, but they weren't going to take my life.*

In the aftermath of injury, rage can be like a racquetball careening off playing surfaces. It can bounce fast and hard, ricocheting from one person to the next—to friends, family members, children, or co-workers—and finally hitting oneself right in the face; or it can lose momentum until it dies by itself. Ned, who sat up at night fantasizing his wife's and her lover's murder, called his in-laws and cursed them. He blew up at co-workers. He drank and got depressed. Finally, the rage settled into raw hatred that then lasted for well over a year.

For the wounded or those who comfort them, rage is an uncomfortable facet of the injury that needs to be accepted, if not expected. People can encourage wounded friends to find the means of expressing rage in the least destructive way possible (screaming into a pillow, for example, or in their cars while they drive alone along nearly empty roads). Rage need not be feared, but people dare not get mired in it, either.

LOVE

Along with rage, the wounded feel love. But the combination of love and rage is like oil mixed with vinegar. Love has been shattered into tiny beads, floating about in a sea of venom. When these beads draw near others, love attempts to reunite them into a whole. The love fragmented by the wound of unforgivable injury is one of that emotion's most odd configurations. Love, in its purest form, does not give way easily to indifference. It struggles to endure just as a dying organism does or as oil in vinegar reorganizes itself. After an unforgivable injury, love is permeated with rage, hate, sorrow, guilt, and impotent pain. Still, it struggles to restore itself into a whole; to survive.

Aubrey, whom I described in the introduction as a client who had witnessed her father murder her mother, professed to love her father even after he had also raped her. She told me this:

> *Of course I love him, and he loves me. Fathers love their children, and children love their parents. That's what the Bible says, and that's how I will always feel.*

Almost all wounded people, including neglected friends, betrayed spouses and parents, and abused or abandoned children, continue (for a while at least) to love their injurers. Love is, after all, not only a feeling but also a habit, and habits are hard to break. Some spouses continue to sleep with their unfaithful partners, for example. Some try to counsel them. Children, more than other groups, relinquish love very slowly. If they let go of love for their parents, where might they find it again? For marriage partners, love is supposed to endure beyond sickness, beyond times of trouble. Although an idealized view, perhaps, ideals are as hard to jettison as habits. Losing your habits and ideals is equivalent to losing yourself. It is hard enough to have been hurt, to have figuratively had a part of yourself blown away; but to give up the remainder of yourself, the love in your heart, is like losing everything. So when people let go of love, they have to feel the full force of an unforgivable injury. They have to grieve over the loss of a history with another person and for a future that will not be. They also have to grieve over the parts of themselves that are gone.

In the aftermath period, if wounded people insist that they love their injurers, comforters should try to understand that if a person hangs on to love, she hangs on to whatever control she has left over the timing of her losses. She will lose belief after belief; but to lose love too soon is to lose the self. And a self intact will be needed if the sufferer is to heal.

HATE

Like rage and love, hate is experienced by injured people directly after they have been wounded. Hate, a cold, bitter emotion that almost seems to invade one's insides, need not be accompanied by a fit of anger, as rage is. Hate can be felt boiling in the stomach or burning in the esophagus or pulsing cold through the blood.

Dave, the man whose mistress left him during his son's illness, said this about hate:

I hated Rebecca for dumping me, and I wanted to hurt her physically or ruin her reputation. Fortunately, I never really tried to do anything. But then I reached the point where I hated everything: I hated the fact that my son was dying; I hated Rebecca; I hated the limbo of being separated but not divorced from my wife. I hated God, and I really hated myself.

During all of this, I got chest pains and had neck trouble. I got intense heartburn. I couldn't sleep. So I started reading the Bible again at night. But I'd just feel dirty.

Hurt people feel hate along with their love; such competing emotions weary the wounded even further. Sleepless nights tormented by hatred and followed by seemingly endless days obscured by exhaustion bring many of the wounded to the brink of collapse.

Hatred is an emotion most of us feel uncomfortable expressing. We are told not to hate from early on in our lives. Most people who are able to forgive, though, come to admit the depth of their hatred. In fact, the admission of hatred is integral to their experience of forgiving. One woman I talked with hated her mother so much she admitted to planning her murder. A daughter whose father forced her to have an abortion described her feelings this way:

I HATED my father. Cold hate. What he put me through was for him, not me. I was in a daze for a long time, you know. I didn't feel anything for anyone. My father didn't speak to me for over a year after that, and I hated him even more. I tried to commit suicide but stopped. I was sick with headaches all the time. I felt sorry for my mother and brother having to live with him.

Because love, hate, and rage are experienced so closely together and because each is such an intense and extreme emotion, the aftermath is a time of frightful confusion and highly charged exhaustion. It is frightening to experience and frightening to watch someone experience. The best that a wounded person can do is attempt to suffer through it; and the best her friends can do is to comfort the sufferer with understanding and acceptance. Sooner or later the symptoms of the aftermath will give way to less complex emotions and to a search for resolution.

Controlling the Aftermath Period

Injured people, for reasons of emotional survival, attempt to find ways to control the damage that is inevitable following an injury. One way I have mentioned is that the recently wounded continue to organize their emotions around love for the harmer. If a person hangs on to love, she can hang on to hope. The same is true for self-blame. If a person can blame herself, maybe she can alter the flow of the injury. Perhaps, a spouse reasons, she can lose weight and that will bring her husband back. Maybe, a daughter rationalizes, she can visit her father with a gift of some kind and this time he will love her. Love and self-blame slow the full force of having to feel the injury and recognize its finality. There are other ways, too, that injured people regulate the flow of events during the aftermath period. They can make demands, beg the injurer to change, become ill or more dependent, attempt suicide, or act out.

Marian acted out when she began to drink with her friends almost every night after her husband left her. Once drunk, she would call him and cry or threaten suicide. For a short period, he came to her rescue; but when he tired of chasing after her and refused to continue, she was forced to accept that her marriage was on the rocks. The method a person chooses to control the aftermath period usually depends on how much power she has over the injurer and what kind of leverage that power provides.

People used to having control over others, when injured, attempt to bring them under control again by selecting some method of enforcement of old rules. They try, in other words, to resurrect the moral contract, wave it in the face of the offender, and demand compliance with its terms. Pilots in Command, especially, use this tactic. Some might be aggressive; others might issue ultimatums; some call lawyers. A few might even attempt physical restraint.

One woman called her pastor and told him about her husband's affair to try to gain some leverage and make him stop seeing the other woman.

> *I was hurt so bad I couldn't take another minute of it. You have to tell someone. Telling would stop it because it would shame him. So I went out and just started blabbing. I called my pastor and said, "Jim is having an affair with Gail." Then I told my husband I had called him. Was he shocked!*

For people who are used to power and control over their subordinates, a direct and assertive method is the most familiar and ordinarily successful way of getting others to do what they want. Just as a parent orders a child to stop misbehaving, the Pilot demands that her injurer simply stop hurting her. In the very worst scenario, such people may become physically violent when they are hurt. More likely, though, when Pilots in Command recognize that their ordinary repertoire of skills at bringing things under control is not working, their sense of mastery in general begins to fall apart. It is then that the flood of pain washes over them in its full devastation.

For people who count on their spouses or others to protect them from harm, the power equation in the relationship is different. Subordinate people have little leverage to bring others back under control. Often, when betrayed, this type of person makes an appeal to the harmer or attempts to appease her somehow. Another approach is for the injured person to minimize the harm or to deny that the injurer was really capable of doing such damage. This latter tactic is common. Wounded spouses, especially, control the flow of pain by inventing excuses for their partners. Often they attribute the unforgivable injury to drunkenness or illness of some kind, as this battered woman did:

> *I have to say, "That happened yesterday. Today is today." You live from one day to the next. I mean, he wasn't responsible. E wouldn't do that. He couldn't help himself when he drank, I thought, so it wasn't intentional or anything.*

Had she admitted intentionality, she would have had to admit that she was injured and that her husband's disposition played a part.

The wife who found out her husband had an affair with a man reasoned that he must have been so ashamed of himself that he might take his own life. Only later did she realize that he had been having homosexual relationships throughout their lengthy marriage.

> *First, I was more worried about him than about myself. I was afraid he'd jump off a bridge or something. You know, he'd say, "What's wrong with me? Why do I have these urges and feelings?" So I was so worried about him that I didn't have time to get angry.*

People who are subordinate to others attempt, as do more powerful people, to use whatever tools they have in order to retain some control over their unforgivable injuries. If bending over backward to please has worked in the past, they will more likely bend further. If sex has worked, they may try that. If begging or crying or getting sick has worked, they might try that. As happens to the more powerful, however, it finally becomes clear to the less powerful that nothing works. The wound is permanent, and all of the old rules are useless.

Children in the Aftermath

Children in the aftermath of injury may attempt suicide, as may some adults. For the powerless, it may seem like the only form of control a person has over anything. This was true of a badly abused teenager who concluded that suicide was her only option. She had told her doctor about the abuse she had endured for years from her parents. As with the girl who told her guidance counselor, it was the first time she had ever told anyone. Although the daughter had nearly died at her parents' hands before, the doctor called the parents, who were prominent people in the community, and told them he was going to report their abuse.

I just panicked. I'd never actively provoked the two of them to hurt me before. When our doctor saw what they'd done, he told me he'd have to report it. For the first time, I feared for my life, but I decided if it came to that, I'd kill myself first.

Suicide for this youngster would have been the way to control her injuries. Fortunately, it did not work. Other children select more typical forms of "flight" or "fight" as mechanisms for controlling pain.

Flight is the attempt to flee from harm, and fight is an attempt to stand up to it. The flight or fight responses unforgivably injured people experience take four major forms. Some children use them all; some only one.

Forgetting or repressing are common forms of flight. People who forget events can recollect them if somebody provides a few provocative details. People who repress events, on the other hand, cannot recollect them even if someone reminds them of the details. Repressing and forgetting are common experiences of wounded people.

A woman whose father raped her throughout her childhood reported that she recalled the attacks, as many Vietnam veterans have reported nightmares and flashbacks about the war:

> *To me, half of forgiving is remembering. I had really started to lose it, so my friend had me hospitalized. Then I was put into therapy with a good psychoanalyst who was also a hypnotist. And it was under this hypnosis that I reported these horrible rapes that went on for years. I didn't remember them at all.*

Another woman, repeatedly beaten and strangled by an older brother, remembered some of those occurrences, but forgot large chunks of her childhood.

> *I don't remember anything about my childhood, really. I remember the third and the eighth grade. I felt special in the third grade. I had a teacher who really liked me. I don't remember why in the eighth.*

Forgetting and repressing for children and adults alike are major mechanisms we use to protect ourselves. When we use them, we flee from harm, if only temporarily. Flight into fantasy provides a similar function.

Many people injured during childhood flee into rich fantasy worlds. Some read voraciously; some escape into art or storytelling. One woman who was an incest victim reported that she made up stories and much later realized that the characters she fabricated represented herself in different situations.

> *At twelve, I started escaping from him. I'd hide or go out. Then, a while later, it was a strange thing. I went on a holiday, and I began writing. (I've always written a lot.) And I realized I was separating what was happening into characters. But those characters weren't at all like me. They expressed emotions! I finally realized they were all me—me talking to me. I was talking to myself and recognizing my own anger and disgust.*

Her fantasies had been a way of protecting herself from harm. Other forms of "fantasy as flight" include writing poetry, acting, or in the worst cases, developing separate personalities. All are methods to gain some control over the flow of damage resulting from unforgivable injury. They work, at least for a while.

The other reaction to cruelty or injury is fight. Fight is also used by both adults and children as a way to control life's events. One method of fighting is exemplified in the woman's calling her pastor to expose her husband's affair. Confronting the injurer and exposing the injury to an outsider are both ways of fighting back. Other people actually fight physically, some getting into trouble at school or becoming troublemakers in general.

Many children flee *and* fight. One young woman, for example, stayed away from home for long periods of time, then felt guilty because she thought her mother needed her, returned home, and then always terminated the visit in a screaming battle. Neither flight nor fight worked because the mother's brutality was still very real.

Summary

Rage, love, hate, self-blame, flight, and fight are all part of the confusing configuration of the aftermath period following an unforgivable injury. The period, like the injury itself, can be terrifying. Yet it is an extremely critical time in the life of a wounded person. For people going through this period or for their friends and family, it is important and wise to acknowledge that the extremes of this period are normal. But it is also important not to remain frozen in the aftermath constellation. To do so is to become emotionally, physically, and spiritually depleted and, more importantly, to allow a single injury to dominate what remains of one's life. When change is permanent, people must change permanently, too. For the deeply wounded there are no other options: They can either change or slowly drown in a deep pool of hatred.

The aftermath period is a period of collecting one's wits, gaining some time, accepting the permanence of change, and determining whether to go on or not. It is the time after which a wounded person must decide whether to seek some better condition or to live out the rest of life drenched in venom and trying over and over again to restore what cannot be restored. Realities, hopes, dreams, and even fantasies snatched away from people because of unforgivable injuries are lost forever. The aftermath gives them time to slowly begin to accept that fact and to start making decisions as to the kind of future they desire.

PART II

The Journey of Forgiving

FORGIVENESS IS THE ACCOMPLISHMENT of mastery over a wound. It is the process through which an injured person first fights off, then embraces, then conquers a situation that has nearly destroyed him.

Forgiving is also a gift given to the self. Once received, the gift of forgiveness releases an injured person from the burdens and shackles of hate. Forgiveness is the ultimate liberator. It is not, however, easily accomplished.

A person ready to embark on the journey of forgiving an unforgivable injury is in for a rocky voyage. In a way, forgiving is only for the brave. It is for those people who are willing to confront their pain, accept themselves as permanently changed, and make difficult choices. Countless individuals are satisfied to go on resenting and hating people who wrong them. They stew in their own inner poisons and even contaminate those around them. Forgivers, on the other hand, are not content to be stuck in a quagmire. They reject the possibility that the rest of their lives will be determined by the unjust and injurious acts of another person. Instead, people who forgive take risks to reshape their lives into something freed from past pain.

Forgiveness is a journey; and a journey is a process. In a regular journey, you pick a place to go, plan an itinerary, and finally pack the luggage and set off. The process involved in the journey toward forgiving an injurer is, unfortunately, not so clear-cut. Sometimes your destination seems obscure. Sometimes the best way to get there is impossible to discern. Still, even if untidy, there is a process to forgiving—one that you can journey through, with specific obstacles you can anticipate and certain stopping-off points along the way. This process will be described in "Part II: The Journey of Forgiving."

The process of forgiving begins at its point of departure, *naming the injury*, and ends at its destination, *the emergence of a new self.* The stopping-off points in between are *claiming the injury, blaming the injurer, balancing the scales,* and *choosing to forgive.* The departure point, naming the injury, will be described in the next chapter. Before that is done, however, several misconceptions need to be cleared up.

Forgiving, once begun, is not necessarily completed. The process does not propel itself. Because forgiving requires people to go through significant personal changes in both their feelings and their beliefs, some may choose to quit short of finishing. Forgiveness does not come about in a quiet, passionless way. It is not like the objective act of a governor's pardoning a criminal. Forgiveness has its passions and its price tags. Unlike a pardoned criminal who is expected to pay no price, an injurer is expected to pay something. A forgiver by no means simply exonerates the harmer from punishment or repayment. If the injurer repays nothing, it is not because the wounded person has not sought compensation. It is because the injurer has refused to comply or, worse, made himself totally unavailable.

Forgiveness is not mystical or impossible to accomplish without the help of a higher power. While some people say God helps them forgive, others forgive alone or with the help of friends. Forgiveness is a rational process; it is a conversion in the way you have thought about yourself and other people and about harm and vulnerability. Forgiveness results in a reconceptualization of the way you believe you fit into the larger scheme of things.

People who succeed in forgiving someone else share two characteristics: At the end of the process, they are liberated from hatred for their injurers, wishing them no harm. Also, once forgiveness is complete, they develop new systems of beliefs about the causes of events in their lives. Their belief systems incorporate an understanding of intimate injuries. Once a person has gone through a process of forgiving the unforgivable, very little can ever seem unforgivable again.

Forgiveness, like all travel, begins with the first step from the point of departure. "Phase One, *Naming the Injury*," is that point of departure. Forgiveness begins when naming the injury begins.

CHAPTER **4**

Phase One: Naming the Injury

> All changed, changed utterly;
> A terrible beauty is born.
> W. B. YEATS, "Easter 1916"

Douglas, Sally, Frank, and Billy Newcomb played baseball in the field next to the creek behind their house. As usual, Sally felt nervous. She had not played very well, and she knew how terrible Douglas's temper could be when she played badly.

It seemed to the other Newcomb children that because Douglas was the oldest, he got away with being mean. Mr. and Mrs. Newcomb turned their heads when he flew into his rages. They had done nothing when Douglas hit a younger sister with a frying pan. So when Sally missed catching Frank's fly ball and saw the screwed-up viciousness on Douglas's face, she knew she would be in trouble later on. She wondered if he would rape her again or choke her, as he had done to their youngest sister.

After Frank and Billy had gone off somewhere later in the day and before their parents came home, Douglas came into Sally's room and silently, with his index finger, commanded her to follow him. His face was red with stored-up fury. Sally went quietly.

Douglas took her to the baseball field, picked up a bat, and used Sally's head as a ball. Then he dragged her to the creek and pushed her head under water four or five times until she blacked out.

When her father carried her to the hospital, he told the doctors she had fallen down the stairs. No one ever said anything about the incident again.

Sally, twenty-seven when I talked with her, described her life of failed relationships and low self-esteem. She said she'd been engaged eight times and had one brief, abortive marriage. Most importantly, she described her need to push love away. If she fell in love and her partner did not, she would feel safe. However, if someone fell in love with her, Sally would become frightened and agitated. When this happened, she would end the relationship.

A number of years went by before Sally grasped the full meaning of what Douglas had done to her and was finally able to identify its effects on her life. Sally realized that she was afraid of the combination of love and sex. Either by itself was tolerable; together they terrified her. Douglas's sexual assaults and other brutality had permanently altered her beliefs about both. The two were mutually exclusive ideas. Once she had "named" the real injury and identified her damaged beliefs, she could begin to forgive.

The first phase of forgiving, *naming the injury*, has one overall objective—to help you interpret the meaning of your injury and your beliefs about it. When you complete the naming phase, you will have come to recognize the scope and depth of the injury you have sustained, from the betraying event that hurt you to the identification of specific damages done to various of your beliefs. Naming helps you isolate what you are going to forgive. Just as Sally Newcomb finally recognized that if she forgave Douglas it would be as much for the damage he did to her ability to sustain intimacy as for his brutality, once you name what it is you must forgive you will also come to recognize its true nature.

The Three Questions to Ask Yourself in the Naming Phase

There are three questions you will attempt to answer during this first phase of forgiving:

1. What were the moral rules that were broken? How did the betraying event break those rules?
2. Have you been a Mathematician (or Pilot in Command or Defenseless Drifter) in your relationship with the injurer?
3. What is the meaning of this injury? That is, how long can you expect the injury to last? What, if any, control do you have over it? What are its consequences?

The answers to these questions will evolve from your willingness to carefully analyze the wound through engaging in the tasks of the naming phase. In other words, you will need to do some homework in this phase, as in all other phases of forgiving. Naming requires that you go beyond the raw emotions of the aftermath period. As you begin the journey of forgiving, you will need to think about the injury as much as feel it. It will be your analysis of the wound that reveals what it is you must actually do to forgive it.

A way for you to begin to consider the full meaning of your injury is to return to the three questions listed above.

To answer the first question—What moral rules were broken?— you will need to assess the nature of right and wrong that evolved between you and the person who harmed you. Who set those terms? How had they been tested? How did the betraying event violate the agreement? If you were a child when you were hurt, what do you think the moral rules between you and your parent *should* have been? Do you think the rules were fair? Did both of you understand them to be the same? Might there have been differences in your interpretations?

When you name your injury, you clearly identify how the behavior of the person who hurt you violated an agreement. Injuries, other than the unforgivable, may hurt feelings, but they do not destroy a person's notions of what is right and what is wrong. You will need, during the forgiving process, to either hold on to your convictions about those beliefs or, later on, modify them somewhat. Either way, you will first have to assess what you believed about right and wrong before you were harmed so that you can redefine or recommit to those ideas later on.

To determine the answer to the second question (Have you been a Mathematician, Pilot in Command, or Defenseless Drifter?), you will need to assess your expectations of other people, especially your expectations of the person who hurt you. Did you expect her to abide by some rigid set of rules—perhaps ones that she had no hand in shaping? Might your expectations have been unrealistic? Unreasonable? You need to reassure yourself that you had a right to expect compliance with the rules you and your harmer chose to govern your relationship. If you determine that you were reasonable in your expectations, some of the confusion and self-blame you are probably experiencing will begin to abate. If you decide that your expectations were unreasonable, you will reassess the causes of the injury in a different light.

The third question asks: What is the meaning of this injury, how long will it last, and what are its consequences?

When you become ill, you want to know what it means. You may ask your doctor such questions as What caused the illness? How serious is it? How long will it last? What, if anything, can I do to help cure it? And how will it affect me? The more you understand the illness, the better able you will be to treat it.

Similarly, if you suffer an unforgivable injury, you want to know what it means. You already recognize that your beliefs about yourself, your intimate injurer, and your world have suffered. Now you want to understand what these losses of beliefs mean to you. Who caused the injury? How long will the suffering last? Do you have any control over its course? Have all of the consequences unfolded, or are more to come?[1] What you decide about the *cause, duration, controllability, and consequences* of your injury will help you determine whether and when to forgive.

CAUSE

During the naming phase, since you are still experiencing the aftermath of injury, you continue to look for reasons it happened. The full exploration of cause, however, is a separate phase of forgiving (see chapter 6). For now, you can trust that until you know more about what has happened to you, you will not be able yet to determine everyone's part in it. Sally Newcomb knew that Douglas had hurt her, but only later did she recognize all that he had done to her and accept his brutal nature and likely mental illness as most responsible for it. Her parents were responsible for not protecting her. Fixing responsibility for an unforgivable injury takes longer than recognizing its duration, controllability, and consequences. Knowing this, you can work to understand the other dimensions of your wound now, as the injury's cause continues to reveal itself over time.

DURATION

The answer to the question about the duration of the effects of your injury is this: You have been permanently affected, but a change in your beliefs need not be negative.

Unforgivable injuries, unfortunately, are not like the flu or some other short illness. They are more like chronic afflictions. Both last a lifetime; both change people permanently. But there is an important difference. Chronic illnesses often end in physical and spiritual exhaustion (although many people gain peaceful and sharpened personal philosophies from them). Unforgivable injuries, if forgiven, will result in a new personal philosophy and in feeling healthy again one day.

When you accept the permanence of the injury, you set the stage for confronting the wound directly and for developing new beliefs to replace the old ones.

CONTROLLABILITY

You have already learned that you were not able to control the injury's occurrence. Nor have you been able to reorder agreements or restore your original relationship with the person who hurt you. Marta, a woman in her fifties, tried for years to please her abusive, violent mother. She was unable to name her injury during those years because she could not see what it had done to her concept of control. A Defenseless Drifter, Marta put her experience this way:

> *I guess I believed that even though she had always been mean to me, sometimes violent even, I could control her moods if I kept giving her things. One time I took an antique tea set to her house. She loved antiques. And—I can still see it—she threw it, a cup and a saucer, I mean, against her porch wall. We were sitting there drinking tea at the time.*
>
> *It took me a long time to realize I could not control her or her moods. In fact, I couldn't control myself even to not go over there and take that abuse from her. What she had done to me was make me think I controlled everything when actually she still had me under her spell when I was fifty.*

When you name your injury, you let yourself see that you are both permanently changed and that you have lost control of the harm you have experienced. Pilots in Command struggle to accept the fact that they are unable to rule their subordinates. Defenseless Drifters try to reconcile themselves to the fact that they cannot count on someone to protect them from harm. Mathematicians give up their equations about injuries. Each type of person must acknowledge that her ideas about control over personal unforgivable offenses must give way to some other set of beliefs.

In the naming phase, you will respond to the question "What control do I have over this injury?" with the answer "Almost none." You can control the fallout of the injury, though, to some degree. You can still choose what to do in your free time, for example, or how to try to manage your emotions on a day-to-day basis. You have not, in other words, lost control of your life. What is out of control is your sense that the moral boundaries of your relationship can any longer be mutually defined with the person who harmed you. Out of control, also, is any likelihood of resurrecting the dreams and hopes about the future as you imagined it.

These are the conclusions about control you will draw from the naming phase of forgiving. The sooner you allow yourself to accept them, the more quickly you might be able to move forward into the next forgiveness phases.

CONSEQUENCES

The most deeply wounding aspects of your injury are revealed in another dimension of meaning—consequences. While even minor events have their effects, those of unforgivable injuries are profound and unsettling because they go to the heart of a person's core assumptions and questions about life.

To whom am I vulnerable?
What kinds of harm can I prevent?
Who deserves to be harmed?
What is justice?

Each person, harmed or not, puts together a belief system in which the answers to the above questions make sense independently and in which the independent answers fit together to form a logical belief construct.

Imagine you answered the questions prior to your injury as follows: You were vulnerable only to your boss. You had control over personal, intimate injuries because you and the important people in your life agreed with each other about loyalty and truthfulness. If people get hurt and it's not an accident, they must have done something foolish. Rewards, punishments, and justice are logical. People reap what they sow. These answers, taken together, form a complete picture of the way you might have thought about fairness and harm. If your best friend, then, has an affair with your husband, each belief would fail, and the whole construct would collapse with them.

Every person organizes her perceptions of the world into an orderly construct in which rewards and punishments are meted out rationally and people are rewarded and harmed with good reason. Most people are not psychologically equipped to accept the world as random or chaotic or to believe that personal behaviors are not necessarily connected to people's reactions to them. For example, if a person in your office is fired one day or a friend takes up mud wrestling, you conclude that there must be good reasons for both. The fired colleague must be experiencing punishment for something she did wrong; the friend must get some reward—applause, perhaps—from her new extracurricular pursuit.

Psychologists call the principles that people construct in their attempt to make unjust events appear to be just *just-world principles*.[2] In a nutshell, just-world principles are constructed because people need to believe that harm has a logical reason. It would be psychologically intolerable to believe that harm is random or a result of some kind of chaotic, inscrutable law of nature. This being so, people construct ideas about justice to give what appears unjust meaning. A person's just-world principles are essential components of her worldview. An unforgivable injury destroys your construct of a just world. It throws it into turmoil, and your faith in justice itself is lost. Here are some versions of some just-world principles people believe in:

> If a man is arrested, he must have broken the law.
> If a woman gets cancer, she might have eaten too much red meat.
> If a man is poor, he doesn't work hard enough.
> If a man leaves his wife, she must have driven him to it.
> If an infant dies, God must have wanted it that way.
> If a man dies of AIDS, he must have deserved it.
> If a country is suffering widespread hunger, it must be God's will.

All of these versions render the world nice and tidy. If bad things happen, in all likelihod, someone deserved it.

The problem with this principle is that when it comes to your own unforgivable injuries, you cannot believe that *you* deserved to be wounded. If you did not deserve to be wounded, what about other injured people? Does this mean the poor man does not deserve to be poor or that the woman with cancer did nothing to bring it about? If a principle about justice does not apply in one circumstance of misery, does it apply to any? The wounded person searches for justice. If no principle applies to yourself, you have two options: You can try to find a reason that you deserved to be hurt, or you can give up your ideas about justice, at least for a while. Usually it is the latter. What an unforgivably injured person admits is something like this:

> *I thought I knew what justice was and how it worked. When bad luck or tragedy came into a person's life, I always thought the person must have done something to deserve it. I did not deserve to be wounded, so I no longer understand how justice works.*

Sam worked for his father and ran a large portion of a business he assumed would one day be his. Suddenly, without warning and for no reason, Sam's father fired him. Sam's wife was pregnant with their first child at the time. Sam looked for a principle of justice to justify his father's unprovoked actions:

> *I knew no one got laid off for nothing. I'd been around the business for a long time. And I'd done a really good job (or so I was told). My father and his accountant had never complained about my work.*
>
> *No one just walks in and says, "Take your stuff out of your desk and collect your pay," when there's no reason for it. I didn't know what the reason was, but everyone I'd ever known who got fired deserved it. So I reasoned, for a long time at least, that I must have had it coming.*

Sally Newcomb decided that her brother's assaults must have happened under some principle of justice. Why else would her mother have allowed such abuse to go on?

> *My mother had been beaten up by both of her parents. She never said much about it, but I did think, even as a kid, that she didn't protect us from Douglas because she knew something awful about us and thought we should be punished. Maybe she knew something about herself that deserved it.*

People's need to believe in justice (and in the fair distribution of life's rewards and punishment) develops into intriguing constructs, each of which makes any appearance of injustice seem logical and deserved. The demise of the just-world principles of unforgivably injured people might be the most painful consequence of this kind of wound. During the naming phase, you will tell yourself that your wound is long-term and permanent; you are not sure of the cause; you cannot control it; and your construct of justice has been destroyed. Not only must you identify the belief you have lost about yourself and your worldview; you must accept that the person who helped to destroy all of this is a person you have loved.

Once you have clarified the meaning of an unforgivable wound, you can see the goals that lie ahead. You will have begun to find out who caused the injury; you will need to bring whatever aspects of your life you can back under your control, you will decide how to use the experience to improve the remainder of your life, and you will have to redefine your ideas about justice. These are the end products of the naming phase: Once you have named your injury you have set the objectives for the rest of the forgiving process.

The Construction of Meaning of an Unforgivable Injury

The meaning of life's events and the beliefs you derive from them are rarely constructed alone. Not only is the way you interpret each dimension of meaning influenced by cultural and social factors, but the overall interpretations of meanings you attach to your life's events are accomplished through collaboration with others.

For example, when you fail your first test in school and attempt to interpret the meaning of failure, you do not do so all by yourself. You probably already know some things about failure in general. You know that our society does not think very highly of losing (an attitude you have no doubt internalized). You know that your classmates in the past have made fun of people who have failed tests. So failure is not attractive. But when you construct the meaning of this particular failure, you find help.

Your parents suggest that you did not study hard enough. Your fellow students tell you that over half the class failed the test. Your older sister tells you she got an "A" on the same test a year before, so you must be dumb. You construct the meaning of this failure with help from others and, as a result, formulate a belief about the reasons you did not do particularly well.

The same process takes place in the daily events of your life. Friends, co-workers, parents, spouses, and children contribute to your interpretation of your experiences—not only the bad ones but the good ones, too. A shared interpretation of a couple's vacation shows how two people's ideas interact to result in one shared meaning.

The couple, Harvey and Carol, view their recent vacation somewhat differently. Harvey says the vacation was so good because all the road maps were in order, the car was tuned up ahead of time, and there were no long, unanticipated detours. Carol thinks of the vacation as wonderful because they had both packed the right clothes, the weather had been great, and they never fought. After their return, Harvey and Carol tell various sets of friends about their trip. When they have told their story several times, each begins to express some of the other's viewpoints. Together they eliminate some details and retell others. When they reminisce alone, they start to share a construct: The vacation was great, their best ever, because each was happy the other had such a good time. All of their careful planning allowed the other to relax. This is how they will remember and talk about the trip for years to come.

The same sort of mutual construction of the meaning of shared events goes on in times of difficulty as well as good times. When people fight or transgress the rules they have drawn with others (at least if they stay together), they soon begin to negotiate the meaning of these rule violations. Just as Harvey and Carol negotiated the meaning of their vacation, unforgivably wounded people attempt in the naming phase to negotiate the meaning of their betrayals.[3] Through discussion, arguments, and attempts to persuade each other, offenders and those they hurt arrive at some shared interpretation of the transgressions one or the other engages in.

Research about the shared construction of the meaning of a transgression has several interesting findings: Offenders try to manipulate those they injure into believing their renditions of injuries.[4] They try to expunge themselves of blame,[5] their main objective being to manage the other person's impressions.[6] People try to get others to think well of them even if they have lied, betrayed, or broken promises. But if people intend for the relationship to continue, both will use the transgression to resolve discrepancies, accept any responsibility that is theirs, and reaffirm their moral contract.[7] This is the process of constructing meaning when two people disagree but a relationship has not ruptured. Even if the mutual construction is manipulated by the offender, when people can talk together about their problems, they have the opportunity to draw conclusions about the causes, duration, consequences, and controllability of their problems together. The offender helps the offended know what to believe or not believe. This is not true where most unforgivable injuries are concerned.

When you are prevented from negotiating the meaning of your injury with the person who hurt you, you have no option other than to try to make sense of it yourself. This can be a lonely, confusing, and difficult undertaking. The tasks of the naming phase make it less so.

The Tasks of the Naming Phase: Admitting, Exploring, Talking

The tasks of the naming phase are admitting, exploring, and talking. Each task helps you interpret your injury and one or another dimension of its meaning so that you are able, even alone, to construct beliefs about it. The central theme of admitting is to acknowledge the duration of the injury. The theme of exploration is to acknowledge its consequences. The theme of talking is to help you interpret all aspects of your wound, including your feelings about it.

TASK 1: ADMITTING THE PERMANENCY OF CHANGE

Because you are not able to negotiate the duration of the injury with your offender, you may try to tell yourself that your life will go on and that you will be the same person you always have been. The injurer will simply no longer be an ongoing participant in your life. Since the person who hurt you is one with whom you have shared moral contracts and written a uniquely personal moral history, your life cannot simply go on as though nothing has changed except that one person or moral relationship as you knew it is gone. Your sense of trust has changed. Your moral history with this person has ceased or will take a new course. The ideas about justice and harm you believed in are now different.

People who are left alone after their injuries try to restore equilibrium to their lives as best they can. After all, even if you are wounded, you must go to work and carry on your daily life as everyone else does. So, in an effort to carry on, you might be tempted to try to bury your feelings and deny the fact that you are changing and must change. It is important in the naming phase (even if you are not able to reason these changes out with someone else) at least to be able to admit to yourself that your life has changed permanently so that you can also admit that you will have to reconstruct your beliefs about justice, trust, and betrayal.

Admitting an injury acknowledges that you have been dealt a damaging wound. The wound is permanent. Admitting also ends some things. Denial gives way to reality. Myths are destroyed. The raw truth about the damage becomes starkly clear. Betty, a woman in her early forties whose husband had left her suddenly for a younger woman, described how she finally admitted one day the full extent of the damage done to her. It came over her like a sudden, inundating downpour.

> *It's hard to say this, but on his birthday, I was driving out in the country. It was a beautiful, warm day, and I was confused and hurting as usual. . . . I'd tried to spend time with a friend just to pass the day, but in the middle of the afternoon, I just needed to get out of there. She probably thought I was crazy. I* WAS—*in a way. So I was driving home thinking of him (I knew he was with his girlfriend), and I started crying. And then it was unreal. It started from my ribs or stomach or someplace. It was like a wail or something. I was wailing like some animal that had gotten shot. And I was aware it was coming out of my throat, but I couldn't do anything about it. It was like it was someone or something else—like I was listening to something die. Maybe I was, in a way.*

It is hard for anyone to admit that part of her has died because of some unwanted circumstances she did not bring about. Everyone wants to control personal changes. The fact is, however, unwanted or not, a wounded person is in the process of changing. When you accept this fact and admit it to yourself, you might be able to let down your guard enough to look at the other meanings that are changing for you.

TASK 2: EXPLORING THE INJURY

Exploration continues to expose the degree of damage done to your ideas about vulnerability, control, and justice. What are the consequences of this experience? In addition, exploring the injury exposes feelings that have been hurt during the remaining unfolding of the injury.

Ann Roland, the hospital worker in chapter 1 who came home to find her husband walking out on her, provides an example of what she learned about herself after he left. First, he surprised her with his departure; then, with the revelation that he had a longtime mistress. She had lost control of her life. Her belief in truth and loyalty, then in predictability, failed. Following this, her faith in her family's caring came undone when they refused to help her financially. She had lost her faith in justice. Her children hurt her when they took sides. She felt old, lost belief in her physical attractiveness, and came to believe that she was a sexual failure. In her mind she was also a public failure who couldn't preserve a marriage: a failure as a life partner. When her work became difficult, she for the first time thought of herself not as professional and efficient but as someone who couldn't cope well under stress. When she called and wept with her friends, she saw herself as pitiful and weak. When her friends became exasperated with her, she thought of herself as a nuisance and an impediment to social occasions. When she realized that her belief in justice had been shaken, she recognized that she now perceived new people she encountered with suspicion. She saw the world as a corrupt, violent place and all the people in it as out to get everything for themselves regardless of the damage they did others. Because Ann's husband harmed her, her whole worldview had begun to fall apart. She needed to stop and get a grip on those of her beliefs and feelings that remained intact. One way to do this is to carefully explore what still remains unchanged along with what has not.

Exploration should be systematic. You can begin the task by asking yourself a series of questions:

1. To what (whom) am I vulnerable?
   To what (whom) am I not vulnerable?
2. What can I control?
   What can I not control?
3. What can I prevent?
   What can I not prevent?

4. What feelings are changed by this injury?
   What feelings are not damaged by it?
5. What still seems just?

The answers to these questions begin to reveal the depth and limits of the injury. They also reveal which beliefs and feelings have remained unmarred.

No matter how vulnerable or out of control you have become, you have to realize during the naming phase that in spite of the way things appear, some things are still controllable. Even if you have been abandoned, molested by a parent, or battered to the bone, you can still exercise some control.

In fact, some people have some control they can apply to their injury. They can take action on it even in the earliest stages of forgiveness. Carol, an abused child who, as a young woman, married a terribly abusive husband, described her exertion of control over her battering husband:

> *Two weeks later, he left for several days again. I knew he would be drinking, and I figured this time he might kill me, so I met him at the door with a hatchet. I didn't threaten him physically, but I wouldn't let him in. He left, but then he came back with his brothers and destroyed the house and beat me. . . . That's when I went out and got an apartment.*

Taking control did not prevent Carol from sustaining further physical abuse, but it did prompt her to make important lifesaving changes. She saw that she still had many strengths.

Because you cannot explore the changes you will undergo as a result of your injury with the person who hurt you, you might have to go through this task alone or with a friend or counselor. Regardless, the sooner you can see the consequences you are dealing with, the sooner you can set your goals for forgiving.

TASK 3: TALKING

Many people take for granted that talking about problems with another person is helpful; others believe that talking about them does no good at all. If talking about problems does not make you feel better immediately, it does accomplish another critical function. Talking helps you begin to construct the meaning of your injury.[8]

People who talk to their injurers about their wounds begin to solve their problems because together they mutually construct beliefs about what happened. Once beliefs are determined, problems can be identified and solutions discussed. If your spouse hits you and then tells you she just started taking medication that sometimes causes erratic behavior, you can decide whether to believe her and how to proceed. Then you can talk out your feelings and together identify ways to prevent a recurrence of her violence. By contrast, if she hits you and then leaves for a month, you are left alone to sort through your feelings, your interpretations of the incident, and any options you may have.

Talking to someone other than the injurer accomplishes some of the same functions as talking to the injurer. Talking to any other person helps you interpret the events in your life and give them meaning. When you hear yourself tell your story and watch people's responses or listen to their reactions, you validate your interpretations and begin to understand what your injury meant.[9]

When Sally Newcomb began to talk, she finally could sort out the dimensions of her experience:

> *Six or eight months ago I began to talk. I told people—no, I told* EVERYONE—*about Douglas and his abusiveness. Probably some people wish I hadn't talked so much!*
>
> *Before this, when I would hear stories about incest, I'd get so angry. But I'd had to keep my emotions at an even keel for so long—not too much of anything. Not too happy. Not too sad. Then I started remembering and talking. And feeling. You have to get your memory back. Then you have to talk—tell someone. I even talked to my mother, and she cried.*

When you talk to someone other than the injurer (perhaps a friend or counselor), you will arrive at beliefs about the wound that are likely to contrast sharply with those of the person who hurt you. But, in the absence of your harmer, you need to decide something about what has happened to you, even if those beliefs are not shared by the injurer or others you know.

Talking to a friend or counselor orders your experience. You identify in your mind how the injury began and how it ended. Talking also helps you see that other people care for you. But the most important aspect of talking is that it allows you to express your feelings while you formulate beliefs about the injury's cause, duration, consequences, and controllability. Once this is done, the persons you talk with can start to suggest solutions if you invite them to. Whether or not you continue to talk about solutions, talking in the naming phase serves its main function: to help you construct your beliefs about what has happened to you so you can move forward.

Summary

To forgive someone, you will need to know what you are forgiving. To forgive a person for cutting your finger off when she has actually severed your arm at the shoulder is useless. In other words, when you forgive someone for injuring you, you should know what the injury is and what it really means for you.

In the naming phase, you construct the meaning of the wound. You admit you are harmed; you explore the dimensions of the injury, and you talk to other people to validate your feelings and impressions. In naming the injury, you also identify the meaning of the injury in terms of its duration, controllability, consequences, and to some lesser extent, its cause. Once these objectives are met, you are ready to move on to the next phase of forgiving because you now understand what you are attempting to forgive.

CHAPTER **5**

Phase Two:
Claiming the Injury

> You can try to run from your own wounds, but you'll leave a
> trail of blood anyhow.
>
> MONA, A DESERTED WIFE

Deborah had learned to live with her father's alcoholism. She
had never known any other way of life. Sometimes he was
violent; sometimes he was not. When he was, everyone was in danger—her mother, her two brothers, and herself.

Deborah's brother, Timmy, was slow in school. Her other brother,
Patrick, was afraid all the time. He wet his bed almost every night.
Twelve years old and the oldest, Deborah had learned to try to
protect them all, but sometimes she could not.

One night the girl heard a terrible fight taking place downstairs.
She got out of bed and, approaching the top of the stairs, heard her
mother's cries more clearly. What she saw never left her memory.

Deborah's mother's eye was out of its socket and lying on her
cheekbone. Deborah picked up a milk bottle and hit her father over

the head until he fell unconscious. Soon after, she remembered being placed in a foster home. Her brothers each went to separate homes. Her mother recovered from the beating but later died from natural causes, and her father moved out of state. Over time, Deborah lost touch with everyone in her family.

As soon as she turned eighteen, Deborah began to hunt for her family. She found Patrick, who had gotten into trouble with the juvenile authorities. She searched relentlessly for Timmy. Ten years later, she still had not found him.

Deborah carried the weight of her father's violence with her wherever she went. She could not forgive her mother for not protecting her brothers and allowing them to be separated. She could not forgive her father for hitting her mother. She carried Patrick's pain when he expressed his own guilt for failing to help Deborah and protect Timmy. Her father's violence became psychological quicksand. The young woman was being swallowed up by hatred, guilt, and confusion.

Deborah could not distinguish what had happened to her from what had happened to others in her family. To forgive, she had to decide what was hers to forgive and what, conversely, was not. She had to accept her own injuries and leave the others behind for her brothers to claim and to forgive, if they ever chose to.

The second phase of forgiveness, *claiming the injury*, is a phase of taking ownership. Because the ripple effect of unforgivable events produces many different injuries, the claiming phase involves disentangling them, then staking out the injury—in effect, filing a title of possession.

Like other phases of forgiving, claiming an injury requires you to engage in certain tasks. When these tasks are completed, the major goal of claiming—to stop fighting or running away from the injury— is accomplished. When you claim your injury, you stop defending yourself against it. You stop denying that your offender has the capacity to hurt people. You accept the permanent changes that result from the offense. You stop rationalizing the behaviors of the offender or providing justifications for his behavior. You give up trying to pretend that nothing has happened. All of your defenses—denial, rationalization, repression, or projection—begin to give way to an honest confrontation with the fact that you are changing. Most importantly, when you claim your injury, you give up trying to manage everyone else's. You accept that you cannot undo your own harm, let alone that done to your children, parents, siblings, or friends. You must forgive your injury, and everyone else must forgive his own.

The major tasks of the claiming phase of forgiving are as follows: First, you must separate your injury from those of other people. Second, you must accept the injury as permanent. You must "take the wound" into yourself and make it a part of who you are to become in the future. Such tasks are called separation and incorporation. Both can be accomplished alone or with help from friends or professionals; but both require active participation in a sort of dialogue with the injury. It is like looking someone straight in the eye and saying, "I see you, I understand you—and [most importantly] I accept you."

Tasks of Claiming the Injury

TASK 1: SEPARATION

The first task of claiming is to say, "This is my injury—no one else's. Other people may have been hurt, too. But I can't do anything about that. I must forgive this injury because this is the one that harmed me." The separating out brings into focus even more clearly the course ahead for the remainder of the forgiving process. It takes time, attention to the tasks, and relief from demands on resources. It must be done, though, whether it occurs right after the injury or many years later, even after people have reached adulthood.

It is a difficult task to separate your injury from the rubble of unforgivable injuries and to begin to claim only the portion of it that is yours. Deborah had her own wounds to claim even though three other people had been damaged by her father's violence. Her mother, Patrick, and Timmy no doubt experienced unforgivable injuries, but each suffered a different one. The reason each injury is

different from everyone else's is this: Even if the same event precipitates several unforgivable wounds, the moral rules violated are perceived differently by different people. More importantly, each
person's perceptions of cause, duration, controllability, and consequences are unique to that individual. So each victim's experience
in terms of the meaning of the wound is his and his alone. Deborah
experienced an unforgivable event when she saw her mother that
night. Patrick, by contrast, experienced it when he was taken by the
county welfare worker to a foster home and his mother did not
protest. Their wounds were quite different.

The first task of claiming your injury is for you to think carefully
about the differences between what happened to you and what happened to someone else. Then you can begin to sort your injury into
separate "injury piles," one being yours to forgive and the others
being other people's.

Sorting and separating an injury is a difficult task, especially if
you, like Deborah and so many other harmed people, have experienced two combined elements. If you have held a protective role
and have had to watch the injury you experience overwhelm others
whom you were to protect, then it is doubly hard to separate your
injury from the wounds of those you tried to keep from harm's way.
Part of your own wound stems from the fact that you could not
successfully keep yourself or others who trusted you from being hurt.

In a divorce resulting from a husband's abandonment, for instance,
the wife's injuries are not the only ones she must contend with. Also
involved, typically, are children, parents, and others who often suffer
unforgivable wounds, as the following list shows:

Wife's Beliefs That Fail
Beliefs about personal values
Beliefs about personal control
Beliefs about trusting
Beliefs about justice
Beliefs about her family's motives

Children's Beliefs That Fail
Belief that parents are together forever
Belief that the world is safe
Belief that mothers are stable
Belief that fathers are loyal and truthful

Grandparents' Beliefs That Fail
Belief that their grandchildren live in a happy home
Belief that they will always have access to their grandchildren
Belief that their child-raising practices were good

The wife's shattered beliefs affect her children's beliefs, which in turn topple the grandparents' ideas of the future. In addition to these losses, the wife is often the one who has to tend to the broken hearts of her children and deal with the accusations and confusion of her parents. Left alone, she has to try to make sense out of their father's actions and interpret them to her betrayed children. Every day, she confronts her own fears plus the fears of everyone else involved. In this way, her injury grows. She sees the effects of the injury, and she must attend to them. So instead of getting better, things get worse. Life can begin to seem almost too hard.

The same is true in situations other than divorce or abandonment. In almost any unforgivable injury, other people the victim loves also get caught in the injury's wake. Deborah had to stand impotently by as her family was broken apart. She had to listen to her mother's anger and pain. Later, she saw the sorrow her brother felt and understood how the entire family had suffered because of one person's illness and violent nature. Even so, her mother's injuries were not hers; neither were her brothers'. When you share another's sorrow, it is difficult not to allow that person's experience to become a barrier to your own decision to forgive. Your inability to separate your injury from someone else's should not stand in the way of healing.

There are several common difficulties people experience when they take up the task. If you were injured during your childhood, for example, it might help you to know that separating injuries is probably a lengthier task than it would be if you had sustained the wound as an adult. Many children are too young at the time they are harmed to have developed a completely individual identity. If identities are unclear, so are the identities of wounded and wounder. Maturation helps to mitigate this.

Another difficulty may be that if much time has gone by since the original injury, memory may be faulty. Over the years, adults wounded in childhood usually have also taken care of many people, engaged in work, and gone on about their adult responsibilities. If they remember being hurt, they probably remember not only the harm done to themselves but to their entire family. An adult looking back at an injury during childhood needs to say, "This happened to me. It is real. It is mine. As a result, I need to forgive ———."

One woman I talked to, Eleanor, was terribly abused by her father, only she never recalled it. Finally, in a session with her therapist, she remembered being raped. She had taken the time to go into treatment because she felt unhappy in general. She had recalled her mother's constant brutalization at her father's hands, but she never remembered any of her own. One day, she remembered. It was on that day that she began to separate her wound from everyone else's and to claim it. On that day, also, she knew it was her father she had to forgive.

Both adults and children may subconsciously resist separating their own pain from that of others because they fear that others will resent their attempts. Claiming signals that a person believes that his own injuries are worth working on and that they are unique. For some people, the assertion that anything about them, even their pain, is unique erupts in guilt. Guilt can prevent some harmed people from separating their injuries from others' because most people so dislike the feeling. When a person separates his wound from those of others, he is saying, in effect, "I have suffered pain different from yours and want to do something about it."

There are also everyday barriers that get in the way of separating injuries into "injury piles." The most common are demands on personal resources and intertwined self-concepts.

Any person in a state of confusion and pain is depleted of the psychological resources he needs to fight back. People who must, at the same time, also meet others' needs as well as their own can find themselves so exhausted that they cannot begin to separate their injuries out from those of others. They need the freedom and time to do this. Roseanne's story is a case in point.

Roseanne was in her early thirties when her husband was arrested one evening at the couple's home. It seems that for a long time he had been writing fraudulent checks at his business. Suddenly, this rather inexperienced homemaker was fending off bill collectors, making business decisions, raising her children alone, and attempting to maintain her family's dignity in the community. She was not only shocked by her husband's character flaws but also overwhelmed with demands on her time and psychological resources. For the first time in her life, she was attempting to function when she was humiliated.

> *All of my prior assets went down the drain. All that work I did for him, and with him—all the pure emotional input—was wasted. Everything was taken away.*
>
> *As I looked to the future, there was nothing secure. My whole life had been taken away for someone else's selfish actions. My good name, personal references, credit rating—my whole future security was ruined. Something was taken out of me. I'm working to get it back again.*

It took Roseanne time to decide what her husband had actually done *to her* that she had to forgive and to separate it out from what had happened to her parents and children after the same event. Roseanne's parents initially blamed her for driving her husband to behave the way he had. They accused her of wanting a life-style that forced him to steal. Although hurt by their reactions, she finally could reason that even though her parents had been insensitive to her, she had nothing to forgive them for. They had to forgive her husband for what he had taken from them. She knew that she could not restore her parents' myths about who her husband was. Her parents would have to grapple with their own losses. Separation of the injury took a long time because Roseanne's resources were stretched to the limit. She *had* to take care of the crises first before she could stop to take in the changes in herself.

The second barrier to sorting out the unforgivable wound is the blurring of boundaries that occurs between people who know each other intimately. A mother, for example, by definition has that label precisely and *only* because she has children. That part of a woman's self-concept could not come about without the existence of children. The same holds true for other reciprocal roles. Husbands do not exist without wives, nor do grandparents without grandchildren. When part of who one is exists only because another person exists, it is natural that self-concepts become defined, in part at least, by other people.

This being so, it is easy for you to experience the pain of someone who, in part, defines you. To claim your injury, you need to refrain from making this mistake.

If your child is humiliated by a teacher, for instance, it is natural for you to empathize with his hurt feelings and to be angry with the teacher. His humiliation belongs to him, though, even if you can sense his pain. If your spouse is cheated out of a promotion because his best friend at work lied, you can empathize and share his disappointment and anger, but he will need to fight his own battles and decide whether to forgive his friend or not. You cannot do it for him.

Any person whose identity is interlocked with another person's needs to break open that lock before separation of wounds can take place. It is not wrong or bad for a person to acknowledge that another person suffered great pain because of the actions of a third party. What may be wrong or bad, at least where forgiving is considered, is if, in acknowledging another's wound, one fails to recognize one's own pain as distinct from all others. A child experiencing a tornado may ache for months because his favorite toy was destroyed. His father may worry silently because he fears for the family's financial future. Both may speak of "the tornado," but each has to claim what was special about the tornado to him. Only then can the actual loss be grieved.

The psychologist Fritz Perls is widely credited with this description of separation:

> If I am I because you are you
> And you are you because I am I
> Then I am not I
> And you are not you.
> But if I am I because I am I
> And you are you because you are you
> Then I am I
> And you are you
> And we can talk.

The struggle to separate "I" from "you" in the process of forgiving results in claiming an injury. It says, "My injury is mine. Yours is yours. When we understand this, we can talk."

In separating out the personal aspects of the wound, in essence the wounded says to himself something like this.

> *When _____ did that, he started a spiral of pain that left many people in its wake. But my injury is my own. It belongs to me and to no one else. Even though I may love others dearly who were also hurt and even if I need to care for them, I must recognize my own losses and grieve them separately. This wound is mine. This pain is mine. It is my wound I must forgive—not someone else's.*

Failing to separate your injuries from someone else's may have become a mechanism you are using unintentionally to control the flow of your own pain. If you focus on someone else's pain, you are not required to experience your own. Not separating your own wounds from someone else's and instead involving yourself in another person's battles may delay your full feelings from expressing themselves, but it also delays your decision to forgive.

TASK 2: INCORPORATION

You can't run from your shadow, and you can't run from your injuries. We are, each of us, a part of our accomplishments, our training, the rewards we have received, and the sheer luck that has befallen us. We are also products of the love, hate, encouragement, and misfortune we have encountered. It is relatively easy for us to willfully take in the good things we have enjoyed and make them into working parts of our daily selves. We bask in our successes, maybe even brag a little. If children do well, most parents feel pride. But it is more difficult to willfully take in the damage that happens to us. Much of the damage people experience is, instead, taken in unconsciously and turned inward into depression or illness, or it may be turned onto others in the form of aggression. No matter which it is, our good fortune or our injuries, we are a composite of all of our experiences—not just the good ones.

To incorporate means literally to take into the corpus—into the body. It means to unite or blend indistinguishably into something already in existence. Unconscious adaptation to harm is natural. It is one of human beings' major methods of survival and defense against being injured. When unforgivable injuries have occurred, however, the incorporation should be done consciously, as soon as possible after the injury, so that the damage from the injury does not all go "underground."

If damage is only unconsciously absorbed into a person's psyche, it can act like slow poison and ultimately become psychologically toxic. Numerous people I talked to reported that they thought they would literally die if they did not forgive their injurer. They had become "poisoned" by their own hatred and grief. The subconscious incorporation of unforgivable damage can produce a terrible sense of malaise. In addition to grief and hatred, it can cause shame—even when there should be none. (Shame, unlike guilt, is a sense of failure at the essential core of being. Shame does not result from infraction of a rule, as guilt does.) Shame results from a sense of falling short as a person.

Even when an injured person has broken no rule, people who

incorporate damage unconsciously, rather than consciously, can feel that they were unforgivably wounded just because they existed and not because of anything they did.

Hannah, a nurse in her thirties, said:

> *My mother had always been crazy. (It took me until I was an adult to understand this.) She always treated me as if I were some kind of animal. She and my father both were professors, and both were crazy. She hated everyone, especially me. She'd say how fat I was, how dirty I was, how stupid I was. I'd never really DONE anything wrong. How was I to know when she forced me to eat off the floor that she was cruel? Years later, I realized I had internalized all of her messages to me. When I accepted that she hated everyone, I started to see that she was really a pretty evil woman. I had to get rid of my self-loathing and focus on her.*

The trick to positive incorporation is that it is done consciously, not unconsciously. To do it consciously, you must have named the injury and then have separated it out from everyone else's. Then you begin to take it into yourself.

People who forgive share two similarities when they incorporate their injuries. First, they begin to make their pain work for them. Second, they begin to look to the future instead of looking back. Making pain work is a deliberate undertaking that keeps the management of damage at a conscious level instead of letting pain unconsciously take its toll on health or mental health. Making pain work, put most simply, is finding something—anything—positive about it. It may seem almost impossible to do when you are in agony, but it can be accomplished.

What *could* be good about pain? Actually, any number of side effects of pain are positive if you really look for them. One early positive effect frequently cited is the kindness of other people. People commonly "come to the rescue" during the aftermath of the injury. Friends, neighbors, family members, even strangers, show caring and support. Much love emerges when people are in pain. But the wounded have to *notice* it—and treasure it. Loving supporters, even those gained from misfortune, are gifts. Many interviewees were stunned by the love they unexpectedly received from other people when they were in a most vulnerable state. Mona, whose husband deserted her, found comfort in her friend.

> *I called a psychologist and went to see her, but she didn't have enough time. She could see me every TWO weeks. And I was coming apart at the seams. One night, I called a hot line and they said, "Be patient." Be patient!*
>
> *So I canceled with the psychologist, and my best girlfriend became like my shrink. It's funny. She almost became my other me during that time. She said, "You have to have faith."*
>
> *She was a fantastic friend. . . . She totally accepted me and helped me realize it wasn't my fault.*

Another positive aspect of pain during the early phases of forgiving is that it frequently gives rise to an unprecedented sense of resolve. Many wounded people reported that they summoned the resolve to stop pain in its tracks and not allow it to further engulf any other unsuspecting victims. Sam, whose father fired him with no explanation, said:

> *He had hurt me and my wife, but not the kids yet. But in some families the hurt goes on generation after generation. Look at Ireland. It's become inbred there. It has to reach a stage where you say, "Enough is enough."*
>
> *No matter how much my wife and I hurt, we decided we didn't want the pain to carry forward. We wanted our pain to bring something better for our kids. I'm not devoutly religious, but it does say, doesn't it, if you are bashed in one cheek, offer him the other?*

When damage is unconsciously internalized, it can do more harm than the original injury. Damage control should be a conscious and active part of incorporating the injury.

Another positive use of pain is that it can bring freedom to try out new experiences. Mona describes the freedom she experienced after her divorce:

> *Oh, I learned how to sail. I did things I wouldn't normally have done. I used to watch TV. Now I never watched TV. I met a man who was a pilot, and I went flying around in small planes. And I was even afraid of elevators! I felt like "If I die, I don't care."*
>
> *I'm afraid of a lot of things. I wasn't afraid anymore. I wasn't healthy mentally, but I was doing a lot. I was free.*

Like most recent divorcées, Mona was unlikely to continue her new life-style, but she learned that she could live a different kind of life if, later on, she chose to. Further along in the forgiving process, people try out new beliefs and new experiences on purpose, but with a more regulated approach and more from choice than chance.

From pain people also learn they have skills they have never recognized before. Roseanne, who ran her husband's business after he wrote bad checks, came to understand her management talents only after her injury had forced her to.

People in pain early in the forgiveness process can also come into more direct contact with some of their basic values. Mona realized she loved life; that was her guiding value. So she clung to it as if it were a post in a windstorm. Other people hang on because of their children and the cherished values they ascribe to their families. Sudden pain clarifies values if an injured person stops to recognize that that is what it is doing.

Pain from unforgivable injuries, even fairly immediately after the major damage has been done, can and does have some positive points. It is like a bitter-tasting pill whose contents ultimately help the damaged person get well. Then you must swallow the pill every day and taste the bitterness. But every time you swallow it you remember that because of it, you have found new friends, rediscovered cherished values, had new experiences, and developed new skills.

If you could sit outside your own suffering and look at it with complete objectivity, you could see the gains you are making out of your injury. Since this is not feasible, it is at least possible to admit that a new self will emerge from this suffering. To complete the incorporation task in a way that results in forgiveness and not extended resentment and hatred, you must say, "I want to be better, not bitter."

Separating and incorporating are the keys to claiming an injury. It is essential to the claiming phase for the wounded to give up the struggle to fight off the changes that will result from the unforgivable injury. Ultimately, a person who succeeds in forgiving must do so from a position of strength. This means that the sooner you can find empowerment from the bad experiences you have endured, the sooner you gain strength over it.

Pilots in Command must begin to find some strength in learning that they cannot control other people or even the total course of their own lives. Defenseless Drifters can find some strength in their ability just to keep going without the guidance of their defender-protector. They can begin to respect their own resiliency and self-sufficiency, as frail as it may seem.

For the wounded whose equations about life have not worked, positive incorporation can begin when they find something good in an equation that is not yet solved. The Mathematician needs to begin finding something good in the fact that everything about life does not follow some pat formula. There are some things in life that are inscrutable; and that itself can be a source of pleasure if it is viewed as a positive part of the bitter pill of injury.

People who forgive ultimately are able to find greater meaning from their injuries. During the claiming phase of forgiving, the conversion from bitter to better begins. Not to sweet yet, but to better. Like the other phases, claiming involves tasks that require active work. Harmed people must say to themselves, "This is your life. What do you want?" Then they need to separate out their own damage from that done to other people, stake their claim to it, and begin to reframe it to work to their advantage. Once this is completed, you have accepted what it is you alone are trying to forgive. As a result, you are ready to move forward.

CHAPTER **6**

Phase Three: Blaming the Injurer

> People are always blaming the circumstances for what they
> are. . . . The people who get on in this world are the people who
> get up and look for the circumstances they want, and if they can't
> find them, make them.
> GEORGE BERNARD SHAW, *Mrs. Warren's Profession*

Annabelle became a novitiate when she was thirteen. She
served the church for over thirty years and during those
years contributed faithfully, although life was not always easy. When
she worked in an inner-city school and marched for open housing,
some sisters in her order refused to speak to her. The same sisters
and others called her a traitor when she tried to adapt another school
to the needs of a neighborhood. Still, she survived. Then came an
imbroglio that she could not transcend.

An older nun, Sister Camilla, was in ill health and no longer
performing church duties. Because their order was not particularly
wealthy, Mother Superior and some other sisters thought that Camilla should move from the convent to a relative's home. Annabelle
was horrified. She offered to share her room with Camilla and begged

Mother Superior to honor what she considered to be the church's commitment to the old woman.

The other sisters became embroiled in the controversy, some taking Mother Superior's side, some Annabelle's. Friends dropped away. Camilla was subtly pushed out to go live with a nephew, and Annabelle left the order in despair and rage.

At age fifty, Annabelle had to start over. For a long time, she did not know whom to blame. The church? The sisters? Herself? She could not forgive her loss of faith in everything she had woven her life around. It took her many months to decide that individual people were to blame. Even though she also came to believe that the church made adults into children, she reasoned that children can distinguish right from wrong. Therefore, if the other sisters were like children, it did not reduce their responsibility for the way they treated Camilla. It was the sisters, especially Mother Superior, Annabelle had to forgive.

To forgive someone, you must blame someone. If no one is to blame for an unforgivable injury, then there is no one to forgive for it.

The third phase of forgiving is *blaming the injurer*. Blaming means that you conclude that someone is accountable for causing something to happen and that what happened is wrong. Until someone can be blamed for an unforgivable injury, you will spin your wheels over and over again in the mire of the injury until you sink in a combination of self-blame, confusion, and rage.

The Bad Rap of Blame

The first two phases of forgiving answer the question What? "What has happened to me? What has been harmed?" The third phase, blaming, answers the questions Who? and Why? "Who hurt me and why did she do it?" Without an answer to these questions, you can be psychologically paralyzed, unable to move forward in life and certainly unable to forgive anyone.

Many people are uncomfortable with the idea of blaming. The

discomfort may result in part from the fact that there are at least three strong and contradictory messages about blaming that influence people's thoughts and feelings:

1. It is not nice to blame.
2. If things go wrong or an individual fails to reach a desired goal, someone must be to blame.
3. Since it is often legally difficult to determine who is at fault in situations such as an automobile accident (or divorce), these kinds of events should be treated as "no fault."

The first message comes to us as children from our parents. The second is ingrained in our culture, which has historically associated competition as a duel between "good guys" and "bad guys." When one individual fails, it must be the bad guy's fault. The third message comes from the insurance industry and legal profession. Their attempts to reduce costs and paperwork make the concept of no-fault accidents or divorce a lucrative and attractive alternative to adversarial proceedings. In any of the three messages, though, blaming is a misunderstood concept.

In general, blame has gotten a bad rap. A wounded person cannot afford to be mired down in myths about blaming. To "accept personal responsibility" for "negative feelings" about being hurt or betrayed (as if there is nothing wrong with betrayal but there is something wrong with the feelings resulting from betrayal) is false and potentially self-destructive. Anger resulting from betrayal is not anger without cause. To not blame someone perpetuates the focusing of a harmed individual on her own feelings instead of focusing her mind on the logic of the injury. Someone can be held accountable for an injury. Someone is wrong. Someone should be identified. Then someone can be forgiven.

What most people fear about *not* blaming others is that if others are not at fault, then the finger of blame might eventually be pointed at themselves. What most people fear about blaming other people, on the other hand, is that blaming is not "nice" or that no one has the "right" to blame others because it seems an arrogant thing to do. We think if we blame someone, we somehow consider ourselves better than that person.

The Objectives of Blaming

To blame someone is, first, to hold that person responsible for causing an event to happen.[1] It is, second, to assert that the responsible person did something wrong.[2] People do not blame each other for good things; they blame each other when bad things happen. So blaming has two steps: First, you must decide who caused something to happen; second, you must decide that the responsible person was wrong—that is, morally wrong. The person blamed has violated a moral rule you had agreed to and is responsible for doing so.[3]

There is no inherent value in the word "blame" or the action of blaming. There is nothing bad or good about blaming. Blaming, in its technical sense, is to hold someone morally accountable.

There is nothing awful about blaming someone for something (unless you blame other people all the time or falsely scapegoat another). Blaming does not necessarily mean that fury is unleashed. Nor does it always involve vicious recrimination. Blaming accomplishes two objectives: (1) It separates you from the injurer, clarifying those roles; and (2) it brings into focus your intentions and those of the injurer where the injury is concerned. It helps you see how all involved parties contributed to the unforgivable injury. (All involved parties contribute to any injury.) Then it helps you to see that while many people contributed, usually only one is to blame. Blaming allows you to begin to focus your attention outward and to search for solutions to the injury.

Blaming, while having no inherent value, is not easy. Finding answers to the questions Who? and Why? is difficult business. Fixing responsibility and ultimately blaming someone represent the phase in the forgiveness process in which you start to regain power.

As regaining power implies, blaming requires that you become involved in your process of healing. Naming and claiming are more reflective and quiet phases of forgiving. Blaming requires action.

Taking action gives people some control over events in their lives.

The first action toward blaming is for a wounded person to decide who, exactly, can be blamed for her injury. Who are the available "targets" of blame?

The Transformation of Blaming: Finding the Target

Getting from the self-blame so ever-present in the aftermath of an injury to blaming someone else takes time and work (fig. 3). As with the other phases of forgiving, there are tasks involved in blaming. Once they begin, the transformation from self-blamer to other-blamer can start. The transformation starts when you decide who, among all people associated with the injury, could be blamed and then identify who must be blamed.

Three targets can be held to blame in unforgivable injuries: (1) the injurer alone, (2) the injured, or (3) a combination of both. There are other people whom you will sift through to decide if they

Fig. 3 Flow Chart of Transformation from Self-Blamer to Other-Blamer

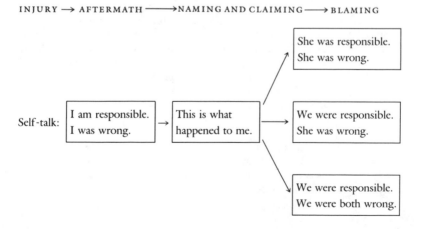

INJURY → AFTERMATH ⟶ NAMING AND CLAIMING ⟶ BLAMING

Self-talk: [I am responsible. I was wrong.] → [This is what happened to me.] ⟶

[She was responsible. She was wrong.]

[We were responsible. She was wrong.]

[We were responsible. We were both wrong.]

are somehow to blame (e.g., in-laws, the "other woman," knowing friends, and so forth). In the end, though, injured people almost always conclude that their injurer, or they together with the injurer, are to blame for the unforgivable event.*

The transformation of blaming means that a wounded person changes from holding herself responsible to holding her injurer at least partly responsible and partly wrong. In the first transformation, the wounded person concludes that the injurer is responsible, wrong, and entirely to blame for the injury. In the second conclusion, both people were deemed equally responsible, but the injurer, who violated a moral contract, alone was to blame. The third conclusion finds that both people were responsible, both wrong, both to blame, and both in need of forgiveness.†

The process of transformation is not cut-and-dried. When an injurer is a sexual assaulter, a thief, or a bold-faced, self-serving liar, it is easier for you to convert from self-blamer to other-blamer. But when people contribute equally (or at least *think* they do) to a situation that results in an unforgivable injury, it may take a long time for you to decide which person did something wrong. This is the end product of blaming. It is also the result of your willingness to engage in the tasks of the transformation of blaming: filtering, weighing, and fact-finding.

* When people assign responsibility to events in general, they usually conclude that either people or the environment is responsible for bringing about a given event. Luck or bad weather, illness, or even some force like God or evil can be held accountable. (For more about the ways people assign responsibility, see H. H. Kelley, *Attribution in Social Interaction* [Morristown, N.J.: General Learning Press, 1971], and K. G. Shaver, *An Introduction to Attribution Processes* [Cambridge, Mass.: Winthrop Publishing Co., 1975.]) In unforgivable injuries, though, it is almost always people who are held responsible by those who are wounded. People violate moral laws: Illness or luck or weather do not, and God does not.
† A fourth conclusion can be that an outside force is thought to be responsible. Alcoholism or mental illness may be blamed for an injurer's behaviors, for example. When this is the case, the injury does not seem unforgivable in the first place. It is more like an accident instead of a moral breach.

The Tasks of Blaming: Filtering, Weighing, and Fact-Finding

TASK 1: FILTERING

Filtering is the first task of the conversion from self-blamer to other-blamer. As the word "filtering" implies, the task requires that you assemble the identities of people who could conceivably be blamed for the unforgivable injury and begin to submit these identities through a "filter" of logic. Once filtered, some people can obviously be eliminated, while some remain. The filtering task is like the task handed to a jury at the end of the closing arguments of the prosecuting and defense attorneys. The jury must sift and filter information and conclude who *could* be guilty and then who *is* guilty. The difference between the filtering of a jury and the filtering of a wounded person is that the jury has to look only at the facts of the case. The unforgivably injured person tends to look at her whole life and the whole life experience of the person who hurt her. This is where the idea of "distant causes" and "recent causes" enters into the filtering task of forgiving.

Every event has distant causes and recent causes. For example, where you are sitting at the time you're reading this is the result of a long chain of distant plus recent events. You may be sitting in your favorite easy chair. You are sitting there because someone designed the chair. A manufacturer made it. You worked overtime one Christmas to be able to afford it. The chair sits under the window in your living room because it was too big to fit anywhere else. You are resting now because the kids are out and your spouse has not come home yet. So there you sit. As you can see, what you are doing right now is the result of a chain of many events to which many people contributed.

The immediate reason you are sitting in this chair at this time might be that you are tired and need a moment's rest before the children get home; but another reason is that a manufacturer made the chair fifteen years ago and you chose to buy it. There are distant and recent causes in any chain of events that lead up to any moment in time.

When chains of events get long, there are links that happened long, long ago and some that happened moments ago. The occasion of an unforgivable injury is no exception. People can think of distant happenings that might have contributed to the cause of an injury and quite recent happenings that might have caused it. The filtering task requires that you sift and filter the distant and recent events associated with the unforgivable injury and decide who can still logically be held responsible. A good example might be the early confused attempts of a recent divorcée to filter her injury as she runs it through distant and recent causes.

If Joe Smith's wife abandons the marriage to take on a new relationship, Joe's thinking might be something like this:

> *Her mother is responsible. She always gave her her own way. When I stood up to her, she left me because I did not let her have her way, as her mother would have.*
>
> *Her best friend is responsible. Her friend had affair after affair. My wife felt left out. If it had not been for this friend, my wife would have been satisfied with monogamy.*
>
> *Her father is responsible. He always had other women on the side. If it had not been for him, my wife would have had a better role model for marriage.*
>
> *Her boss is responsible. He made work so stressful, my wife needed to do something completely irresponsible to cope with the stress.*
>
> *I am responsible. I have been more involved in my work lately than I should have been. No wonder she had an affair.*
>
> *My wife is responsible. She lied. She broke our marriage promise. She took advantage of me.*

From this kind of list, the wounded person will begin the task of filtering.

Filtering does not identify who intentionally hurt you or who broke a moral agreement. It does not, in other words, identify who *should* be blamed. The filtering task lets you generate a list of everyone associated with the injury so that you can begin to think logically about who *might* be blamed. Filtering results in a sort of snapshot of the players in an unforgivable injury. Once the players are identified, the part each played in the injury can be explored. Some can be cut from the snapshot, some can remain there, and some can finally be held responsible.

The next task, weighing, reveals who is responsible and who is not.

TASK 2: WEIGHING INJURIES ON THE RESPONSIBILITY SCALE

The next task in the blaming phase is to decide who is most responsible for causing the unforgivable injury. The responsible parties have emerged through the filter; now the most responsible person must be identified. It is almost always the person most responsible who must be forgiven.

How can you decide who is more responsible for bringing about an event? In other words, what does being responsible for something actually mean?

"Responsibility" is a complex term. In any situation in which people create an event, one person is probably more responsible than another for bringing about that event. Responsibility is a *scale* concept.[4] One person can be high on the scale and extremely responsible for bringing about some circumstance; another can be low on that scale, minimally but still partly involved in the circumstance. People evaluate each other's levels of responsibilty all of the time. After a wonderful dinner party you might ask a friend, for example, whether she thought the success of the party was due to the charm of the hostess or the chemistry of the guests. Who was most responsible? You might argue amicably for quite a while over the question. After a brawl you witness on a street, you might decide the brawlers were more responsible for the fracas than the bystanders who egged them on. You may even report your conclusion to the police.

Determining levels of responsibility is an everyday occurrence for most of us. The irony is, though, that most of us do not fully understand how we arrive at our own conclusions. Weighing is the task that helps you see how and why you decide who is actually responsible and blameworthy. Weighing can be thought of best as follows:

Imagine that the responsibility scale looks like an old-fashioned scale at a meat market. The weight of a piece of meat placed in a pan is marked by a pointer that moves up and down on a vertical arm. The arm is calibrated with weights—the more meat placed in the pan, the higher the pointer goes on the calibration arm. Like the meat scale, the responsibility scale indicates the weight of responsibility—the more responsible one is, the higher the pointer moves on the scale. People involved in deciding who is responsible for something figuratively estimate how high the pointer goes on the arm of the calibrated responsibility scale.

The scale of responsibility has calibration marks at different levels.* At the level of minimal responsibility is the "contribution mark." If you are associated in any way with an event, the pointer would put your place on this mark. Sister Camilla was minimally responsible for Annabelle's departure from the church because Camilla happened to get old.

The next two levels are the most important where unforgivable injuries are concerned. Placing a person on one of these marks makes her more responsible than others who are assigned to the lower level. Once an injurer can be assigned to one of these two higher marks, blame can be assigned as well.

The level above the contribution mark is the "foreseeability mark."

To foresee means to anticipate beforehand that an event will occur. For example, if you know you have a low alcohol tolerance and get drunk easily but go to a party and drink ten cocktails, you could

---

* This scale is a simplified version of Fritz Heider's five levels of personal responsibility for action. For a more complete discussion of levels of responsibility see K. G. Shaver, *Introduction to Attribution Processes*, and K. G. Shaver, *The Attribution of Blame: Causality, Responsibility, and Blameworthiness* (New York: Springer Verlag, 1985).

have anticipated that you might get drunk. You hold yourself responsible because you could have foreseen getting drunk.

If the hand brake of your old car has been broken for two years and it slips out of gear easily, you can foresee that if you park it on a steep hill, the car may slip out of gear and roll down the hill. Should that happen, you'd hold yourself responsible for your demolished car because you might have known that the car would slip out of gear. You did not intend it to, but you could have foreseen it.

You might be upset with your children for playing catch near a neighbor's house. When the ball finally breaks a window, you yell, "You should have *seen* that would happen!" We hold people responsible when we believe they might have known that when they acted a certain way, something specific would result.

At the level of foreseeability, injured people can hold their injurers responsible when they conclude that the injurers could have seen beforehand that their actions might result in injury. If one party in a moral relationship knows that her action might breach the relationship, she can be held accountable for the breach at the level of foreseeability.

Joe Smith thought about his wife's mother, father, boss, and best friend. He systematically asked himself whether any of these people could have foreseen that their behavior could result in the ending of his marriage. After carefully weighing all the facts, he decided that they could not have. Each may have contributed to his wife's attitudes, problems, and unhappiness, but none was responsible for her infidelity. She, on the other hand, was; and she might have foreseen that infidelity could destroy her marriage.

Annabelle held Mother Superior responsible at the level of foreseeability after she concluded that the latter could have foreseen that if she evicted Sister Camilla, even after Annabelle protested, Annabelle would be forced to leave the church.

We hold ourselves responsible when we can foresee the results of our behavior. We hold other people more responsible when they can foresee events more clearly than we can. We hold people even more responsible when they intentionally cause something to happen. Those who intentionally cause an unforgivable injury are most responsible for it. The highest level on our responsibility scale is the "intentionality mark."

Intentionality means that a person knows that if she takes a certain action, a given result will occur. People intentionally lie out in the sun to get a good tan. They intentionally go to work to finish a project or to make money. A teenage boy might intentionally go to some location where he knows a certain girl he is interested in is likely to be. We may intentionally scold our children to teach them a certain lesson.

Intentionality goes beyond foreseeability. A man whose car runs out of gas on a blistering hot day might have foreseen that his long walk to the gas station in the sweltering sun would result in a sunburn. He certainly did not intend to get sunburned, though. A woman who drives under the influence of alcohol and who hurts someone might have foreseen that she could hurt someone, but she did not set out with the intention of doing so. A person who intends to cause an event and who then actually causes it is more responsible than anyone else on the scale of responsibility. The pain caused may be no worse than the pain other people caused, but it was intentional. The pain caused by others on lower calibration marks was not.

The next part of the weighing task is to decide if anyone intended the unforgivable injury to happen. This assignment can be tricky; but once it is accomplished, the target of forgiveness has been found.

People who know each other well can eventually foresee the effects their behavior is likely to have on another person. A husband who throws his wet towel on the floor can foresee that his wife will chastise him for it and insist that he hang it up. A wife who stays late at the office for the third consecutive night might anticipate protest. Husband and wife or parents and children may know each other so well that they can precisely foresee the effects of their behavior on each other. Let's say, though, the workaholic's husband decides to leave the house because he is sick of her absence. As he is wandering about, he meets a woman in a bar and agrees to meet her in a motel the next afternoon. Is he more responsible for the tryst than his overworked wife? These kinds of questions are the stuff of many a mud-slinging argument, the kind that goes like this:

"You did that."

"If you hadn't said this, I wouldn't have done that."

"Well, if you had not done that, I wouldn't have said this."

This is the kind of fighting that people engage in when they try to identify a chain of events that lead up to a certain major injury. Each person argues that the other should have foreseen the injury. Left alone, the injured person often becomes trapped in her own imaginary replay of this dialogue between herself and her injurer. First, she holds herself responsible because she could have foreseen the other person's response. Then she holds the other person responsible for knowing her well enough to see what might happen. Then she holds herself responsible again—back and forth—until she considers intentionality. Who intended to engage in activities that *violated a moral rule* between two people? Who intended to engage in activities that would result in a moral breach or a betrayal of faith? Usually, only one person, and that person is the injurer.

Intentionality in unforgivable injuries has two separate components. The first is that one person intended to take action that might result in the injury; and the second is that the action was wrong. The action violates a moral rule between people.

Here is how Jenny, after being abused for years, finally reasoned out her role in the abuse to conclude that her husband was more responsible and to blame than she was.

He was so cruel. Shockingly cruel. Some people were surprised I didn't kill him, I think. In fact, my doctor said I had one of the worst lives anyone could have. But he was a habitual drinker— not a daily drinker, but every six weeks or so he'd get drunk for a week or so. Over the years, he left me and our children in fear, poverty, and degradation. And yes, I felt terribly sorry for him at times. He put himself into treatment for alcoholism, but he was just as violent sober. Then they diagnosed him as manic-depressive. I couldn't leave; there wouldn't have been enough money. But that made me responsible for the beatings I took.

I finally decided, mentally ill or not, alcoholic or not, he was an intelligent man—intelligent enough to know when he was wrong. I was clever, cleverer than he. I know how to keep things from completely falling apart. But he was wrong. And he knew it. Finally, I said, "If you don't stop this, I'm leaving and serving you papers." He stopped; I stayed. He did, after all, try to help himself. He was mentally ill. And I still cared for him.

Intentionality in the realm of unforgivable injuries applies to the breach of a trust and a contract. Even if you can foresee a certain behavior will probably provoke a reaction, the reaction should not be one that breaches trust or violates a moral agreement. If, for instance, a husband diapers the baby sloppily, he might anticipate a complaint. Complaints do not violate rules of most marriages. On the other hand, if his wife were to respond by stabbing him with a steak knife or unleashing a vitriolic verbal assault that goes on for hours, in all likelihood it would break some moral rules between them. The wife is to blame, even though the husband might have foreseen that his sloppy diapering would provoke a negative reaction. In a similar way, Annabelle could not blame Mother Superior for intentionally forcing her to leave the church. No one intended to force Annabelle out; but Mother Superior might have seen that her treatment of Camilla would provoke Annabelle's departure.

The general rules of fixing responsibility for an unforgivable injury, then, are these:

1. If the injurer's action intentionally breached a vow or promise or violated another moral rule, the injurer is to blame. This is so even if the injured person might have foreseen some of the consequences.
2. If both people could have foreseen that the consequences of their behavior would strain their relationship but only one did something wrong, the person who took the wrong action is still more to blame.

These are especially important points for people who were injured as children. Many times children know that if they behave a certain way, they can foresee the harmful results. For example, a child might be sitting in her mother's favorite chair when the mother comes home drunk. The child knows that if she sits in that chair, she can be hit, but she has not expected the mother to return so soon. When the mother comes home early and beats the child up, the child blames herself. As an adult, the abused person can begin to reason that even though she sat in the chair and could have foreseen her mother's brutality, she was not as responsible as her mother for the beating. Her mother intended to do harm. The child did not. Her mother was to blame. Her mother is the one to be forgiven.

TASK 3: FACT-FINDING

What if you cannot weigh out the most responsible person from those less responsible for the injury? What if even after you have looked over all of the evidence to discern who could have foreseen the injury or which person intended it, you still cannot place blame? This happens sometimes, but not often. When it does, you can take on task 3: fact finding.

Fact-finding usually seeks one answer: Has the injurer ever committed the same unforgivable injury before or since? In other words, is there *consistency* in the behavior? When there is consistency, there is often intentionality. If a person has lied to others, had other affairs, or broken other promises, those activities are part of that person's pattern of behavior. They are not aberrations or mistakes. It is just that in this instance the injurious behavior has surfaced where others could see it.

Nancy, whose fourteen-year-old son died of a self-administered teaspoon of poison, did not believe that his death was a suicide. She suspected that he had taken the poison to make himself sick in order to avoid a confrontation that had been brewing since Nancy had questioned him about his early-morning absences on the day of his death.

For months afterward, Nancy tortured herself with suspicions about the role a young woman in her employ might have played in her son's death. She told her husband of her increasing conviction that the woman had seduced her son, whose fear of imminent discovery she felt prompted him to take the poison. Her husband, however, grew increasingly distant and exasperated with her. He wanted to forget the incident and move on with life.

With her mind working away in a vacuum, Nancy sometimes felt she was going crazy. Finally, she decided that if she could prove that her employee was having affairs with other teenage boys, it would confirm her belief that her son did not intend to kill himself, only to shift his parents' attention to something other than his relationship with the woman.

Nancy called a friend in a detective agency who agreed to call the woman in. The detective was able to find out, just as Nancy suspected, that the employee had had sex with a number of neighborhood boys and even her husband's friends. (He had been overseas at the time.) When Nancy verified that the woman had a consistent pattern of sexual exploitation, she expressed her relief in this way:

> *My friend thought that if he told me that my son had been to bed with her, he was going to destroy my vision of my son.*
>
> *I said, "Good heavens, what did you think I thought he was? What you've really done is given my son back to me." Because, although I really knew what happened, at the back of my head I was thinking, why didn't I let him have a guitar like he wanted for his birthday? Why did I have to tell him he was going to have to pay for his own summer school 'cause he'd flunked algebra and the teachers told me he could've easily gotten an "A"? So when my friend told us that everything was exactly the way I thought, for the first time, my husband believed it was the woman's fault.*

People have patterns of behavior. There is consistency in an injurer's behavior, just as there is in most people's behavior. People continue to blame themselves for injuries, even after the shock has worn off, because they know their own patterns of behavior better than the injurer's. Fact-finding usually reveals that the injurer was behaving consistently with patterns in the past, only those patterns were concealed. As the old saying goes, "Once a liar, always a liar."

Blaming results from the completion of three tasks: filtering, weighing, and fact-finding. Filtering identifies anyone who could conceivably be held accountable for the injury; weighing reveals who is most responsible and to blame; and fact-finding provides information that can help place the injurer on the scale of responsibility. Those tasks accomplished, the injured person has completed the transformation from self-blamer to other-blamer and can proceed to forgive.

Different Blaming for Different Blamers

The ease of blaming other people differs from ethnic group to ethnic group and from country to country. Women may blame differently from men, especially when it comes to failures. Women tend to blame themselves for failures more than they blame other people; men tend to do the converse.[5]

Self-esteem also has to do with whom one blames. A person of low self-esteem is more likely to blame herself for failure than a person of high self-esteem.[6]

Children might also have trouble blaming parents until after they have reached adulthood. Ideas like intentionality or wrongness may be too hard for a child to grasp. This is one reason that many people who were harmed in childhood do not forgive until they are adults. It takes maturation to blame someone else and thereby to identify who really must be forgiven.

Ethnicity, nationality, gender, self-esteem, and age factor into the tasks associated with blaming.[7] Still, to forgive another, you must hold someone else accountable and move through the transformation from self-blamer to other-blamer.

Summary

Many people try their best not to blame. Many think that turning the other cheek means not to blame when it actually means not to harbor ill will. Blaming may seem uncharitable or unloving. Friends may tell wounded people to get on with life, not knowing that blaming is part of getting on with life. In random injuries like lightning strikes, it may be unimportant for the strike victim to insist on knowing why lightning struck. When one is wounded by a loved one, though, you need to know why, if for no other reason than to avoid repetition of the injury in the future.

Some people also might have trouble blaming because of their ideas about rugged individualism. If something goes wrong, they simply "take personal responsibility" or "pull themselves up by the bootstraps." If unforgivably wounded people could do that, they probably would. But most people are too hurt and too confused to square their jaws and march on. They need help, and they need license to blame.

Friends and professionals may have bought into the myth that all injuries are "no-fault." These people may be uncomfortable with anger and the fear that blaming might cause uncontrolled rage. They probably also do not understand that responsibility and blame are not the same thing and that there are many levels of responsibility.

People need to be able to hold someone responsible for their injuries. They need to be able to accept that the wrong done could have been foreseen or was even intentional. Someone is to blame for hurting a person badly. It may be the injurer; it may be a combination of contributions by both the wounded and the wounder. Nevertheless, until confusion clears and the injurer can be recognized, there is no one to forgive.

There is nothing wrong with blaming. In fact, it is good and necessary as long as it is an aspect of forgiving and not an end. The blaming phase is just that—a phase. It should not be feared. Nor should the blamer be discouraged from it. Through blaming, light is thrown upon the injury. The tasks ahead become clear, and the possibility of forgiveness shines at the end of a once-dark tunnel. Injured people need to be told that blaming is a positive step forward—not a place to land and stay by any means but a step on the way to healing. Once you can blame, you know whom you must forgive. When you resolve the identity of the person to forgive, you are closer to accomplishing that goal.

CHAPTER 7

Phase Four:
Balancing the Scales

> I was not going to get vengeance. What could I do to get revenge? If I didn't get revenge, I had to get something.
>
> ANN ROLAND

F red was a lawyer; Yvonne, the director of a social service agency. Together they had a comfortable income. They enjoyed a life of the arts, travel, and nice things. They had no children. Each month, the couple's paychecks were automatically sent to their bank. Fred's went into their joint savings account; Yvonne's, into their joint checking account. It was Fred's task to write checks to pay bills; Yvonne paid scant attention to financial matters.

Yvonne wanted a new car. She had driven a blue Toyota for four years and drooled over Fred's new red BMW. Fred told Yvonne that there was not quite enough money in their savings account for a new car right then but soon there would be. After six months went by with Fred still reporting there was too little money, Yvonne grew disturbed. She decided to examine their bank accounts. When she did, she was flabbergasted.

Yvonne's checks had been automatically deposited into their checking account, but Fred's had not gone into savings. In fact, there was almost no money in the savings account.

Yvonne confronted Fred, and he confessed. About a year and a half earlier, he had opened a separate personal account and had his checks deposited to it instead of to the joint account. From this new account, he had purchased a sailboat that was now docked at a friend's lakefront cabin. Fred and Yvonne's fifteen-year marriage broke up soon after. Yvonne got half of the property and half of what little remained in their joint accounts. The sailboat had nearly depleted Fred's personal account, so little cash was left for her. (His lawyer had managed a way for Fred to keep the boat.)

Yvonne's life-style changed dramatically. She was forced to cut her expenses. She took few vacations and seldom ate out. She also continued to drive her old blue Toyota. It was not until she was able to buy a new car two and a half years after the divorce that Yvonne could begin to consider forgiving Fred.

The fourth phase of forgiving is *balancing the scales*. Balancing the scales has the effect of restoring to the forgiver some of the power or resources that he lost because of the unforgivable injury. Forgiving comes from a position of strength, not weakness. So, a person who is finally able to forgive another must somehow arrive at a place of strength. A forgiver must believe, at least, that he is as strong or has as many assets as his injurer. It is this fourth phase that finally equalizes the balance of resources in a relationship thrown badly out of balance. What do I mean by resources out of balance? To answer that question, we need to reexamine the notion of intimate relationships in general.

Relationships in Balance

Relationships between friends, between spouses, and between parents and children are built on trust, love, habits, sharing of information, and resource management and exchange (among other things). Sometimes one individual brings more into a relationship, or one takes out more, than another. Each relationship finds its own balance so that it can continue to function.

This balance implies that in any intimate group of people, the behavior of each person somewhat depends on and relates to the behavior of everyone else in the group.[1] When one person changes, everyone else must adjust slightly to keep the "system" intact.[2] For instance, if a husband who has not worked for some time returns to the work force, his wife and children will have to take over some of the jobs he had previously done around the house. Or if an adult child decides to confront his parents about the ways they mistreated him as a boy, the parents will have to either listen more or learn to escape his confrontations. Adjustments in individual behavior are the regulatory methods a system uses to maintain its existence. Thinking about marital relations or friendships as kinds of business enterprises might be instructive in showing how a system maintains balance.

A small business enterprise is made up of people who are expected to bring resources to it. These resources may be business know-how, community contacts, collateral, or even a whiz-kid knowledge of computers. Regardless, everyone is expected to contribute what he knows to the betterment of the business.

Inside the business, each person is expected to share resources with the other business partners. One person helps another program a computer or make a necessary contact. No one is expected to hoard resources for his own advantage.

Finally, the small enterprise delivers a product of some kind, and presumably, all are rewarded for their hard work as profits are shared.

Intimate relationships are similar. In marriages, friendships, or parent-child relationships, each person brings some resources to the relationship. Then people share these resources. Finally, something is produced. The product may be only a child's work in school or maybe a family's contribution to a church or community project. No matter what it is, though, the unit works together. No one benefits more than another, if, that is, the system is *fairly* balanced.

In marital relationships people may bring money, nurturing, humor, new information, secrets, troubles, and a myriad of other resources to each other. A husband may bring good humor and an income; a wife, a business mind for managing money and love for a good joke. Together they form a compatible and fairly balanced relationship. The same is true for friendships in which one friend may provide a listening ear and the other a good time. Parents feed, clothe, and shelter their children and provide comfort and guidance; children may bring new ideas, love, fun, and innocence to their parents. As relationships mature and change, different resources come into and go out of them; but the balance still must be maintained between people. If there is fair balance, no one can cheat or the relationship will become one-sided. Unforgivable injuries destroy the fair balance in relationships in the most vital of ways.

Unfair balance in an intimate relationship usually does not take the form of one person's making financial gains at the other's expense (although it does happen occasionally). In unforgivable injuries, fair balance is usually destroyed when one person takes *choice* away from another while at the same time increasing his own. Choice, in addition to love and trust, is one of the most critical resources in an intimate relationship.

Choice can be taken from people in three ordinary ways: One person can deprive another of physical freedom, one can withhold information from another, or one can lie to another. Any of these methods of depriving another person of choice is part and parcel of an event that prompts an unforgivable injury. Sexual assaults, battering, locking people in, or forcing them into hospitals are examples of one person's depriving another of the choice of physical freedom. People can even deprive others of choice in situations where together they should be having fun. If you have fun night after night while your partner stays home doing housework, your partner has lost choice over how to spend free time. Fun is out of balance (unless the one at home thinks housework is fun).

Fred's secret from Yvonne is an example of how choice was abrogated because of withheld information. Yvonne lost the choice of whether and when to buy a new car.

Lies deprive people of choice in another, subtle way.[3] Lies make it nearly impossible for you to make a reasoned choice because your options have been obscured. If someone lies when he professes love to his wife, for example, the wife cannot choose to leave what is, in honesty, a loveless relationship. Stephanie, the woman whose husband had had affairs with men throughout their marriage, said the following about the effects of his lies:

> *I couldn't live with the lies. The last three years of my marriage had been based on a lie. What really scared me, and still does, is that he could have given me a disease—AIDS, herpes, hepatitis. How* DARE *he do that to me!*
>
> *I would have used condoms, or I could have left him or made him get an HIV test. Who knows how this might all end up? But his lies might hurt me longer than his unfaithfulness.*

The events that precipitate unforgivable injuries deprive people of choice; and most people remain in relationships only so long as they believe they can choose from as many options as the limitations of the relationship allow. Since choice, in addition to love and trust, is a critical resource in any voluntary relationship, when one person restricts the other's options while he maximizes his own, the relationship becomes imbalanced. Balancing the scales returns power or resources to a wounded person because it restores that person's options and helps him to believe that fairness has returned to his life.

Since most people struggle alone to forgive without the participation of the offender, trust in the offender is almost never restored. The injurer is gone. Love is rarely restored by forgiveness. Love may return to a damaged relationship, but it will be a different love. By contrast, if it restores anything, forgiveness restores choice. Once the scales are balanced, a wounded person has the perception, at least, that his life has once again become fair. Any unfairness caused by the unforgivable injury is over. Yvonne was able to buy her new car because a new friend helped her out with a loan. The new friend reinforced Yvonne's belief that life was fair again. Then she could think about forgiving Fred.

Tasks of Balancing the Scales

The tasks of balancing the scales are different from those in claiming or blaming. They require even more activity than those previous phases. And the activities are intentionally directed toward empowerment, not more understanding. There is no more to understand about the injury. It happened. It changed your life. The blame has been placed. It is time to move ahead. The goals are to gain strength over the injury. The tasks give you that strength.

Depending on who you decided is to blame for the injury *and* whether the injurer is available or not, the tasks of balancing the scales are selected from a menu of four possibilities, each having the effect of increasing your personal choices.

1. To consider the injury over and done with and move on to the next phase
2. To punish the injurer
3. To load resources to your depleted reserves
4. To mock-punish the injurer

You may select more than one task if you choose. Whatever is chosen, however, should empower you and put you in a position of strength.

POSSIBILITY ONE: CONSIDER THE INJURY OVER AND DONE

If you concluded in the blaming phase that you and the injurer both are responsible and to blame for the chain of events that damaged your relationship, you are left with two options: You can continue to blame interminably, or you can consider the injury over and done. Joan, who played a joke on herself when she mentioned divorce to her husband and he took her up on it, selected the latter option:

> *After you've said things to people, you can never take them back. Once you admit you hate someone, it's the beginning of the end.*

Once you hate someone, you know things can't be restored. I had to accept it. My life had changed. But when I looked at it, we had just started drifting apart. He HAD been a good husband. He did a lot of work in the house. He had been good with the kids. He was reaching a point in his life where he was stuck in his career and knew he wasn't going to go any further. He was sick of remodeling. And, he was saying, "I'm going to go out now and start doing the things I never did before."

So we had both come to that mid-life with change in mind. But the change took us both in different directions. I wish we knew as much as we do now. He told the kids if he had known that their mother was just trying to scare him, we'd still be married today.

So I had to look at the divorce and not blame him for every-thing. I had to come to terms with my own part in the fail-ure . . . and then I had to accept myself as a sinner, too. I had done wrong things, too. I also knew that if God forgave me for being human, I had to forgive him for being human, too.

If you draw the conclusion Joan drew, you accept that you, along with your harmer, are flawed and faulty humans, each capable of doing harm. You actually forgive humanness rather than a particular harmer. This is ordinarily not what happens during the process of forgiving, though, because most people rightly conclude that the one who hurt them did so to gain personal advantage at their expense. (Many people do finally draw the conclusion that all people are equal in their capacity to harm others, but this new belief is ordinarily a *result* of forgiving a terrible betrayal, not a part of the process. Yvonne, for example, did not consider herself as duplicitous as Fred because she, in fact, was not. Yvonne was an extraordinarily honest person. But years later, after she took stock of some of her own frailties, she had more empathy for his.)

The acceptance of your own wrongdoings or frailties is a humbling and sometimes painful experience. It takes a big person to engage in the kind of self-analysis that is likely to result in the conclusion that you were equally to blame for an injury that altered your dreams and broke your own heart. The first step might be the acceptance of self as a person who is perfectly capable of harming others. The next step might then be to accept that the "self" could have foreseen the injury coming.

Joan explained how she looked herself squarely in her bitter face and recognized her own capacity to hurt others:

> *After four days of crying, I said to God, "Here I am, help me." Then I started making up a lifelong list of harms I had done to other people. I went back to kids in grade school. Friends in college. Everyone. And after I was done, I lay down and slept for the first time in days. After that, things started to change. I began to see my part in the responsibility for the divorce.*

To accept equal blame, then, you must acknowledge that you were responsible for bringing about the injury, that the things you were responsible for were morally wrong, and that you probably could have foreseen that your behavior would bring about the painful situation that occurred.

This self-searching for equal blame is one task on the menu for balancing the scales. It does not mean that you accept *more* blame than the injurer but, rather, equal blame. Once you arrive at this conclusion, the choice to forgive is available.

POSSIBILITY TWO: PUNISH THE INJURER

A more frequent fact about unforgivable injuries is that the injurer is to blame. He either intended the injury to happen or could have foreseen it. He also knew his actions violated a moral contract. When an injurer is solely to blame, he has also taken resources from someone else without that person's knowledge. Self-interest is the driving principle. In this case, a common method people I talked to used to balance the scales was to punish the injurer.

Punishment, like blaming, should not be confused with revenge or recrimination. There is a very fine line between revenge and punishment. Revenge comes from deep rage that is released through taking punitive action. A person seeking revenge asks, "What can I do to feel better, to get some relief?" A person seeking to punish, on the other hand, is searching for a way to teach a lesson. A punisher is looking for a way to remind an offender that he has violated some rule.[4] Punishment lets a person know what he did wrong. Revenge does not. Punishment is fair and instructive. Revenge is not.

Punishment is a method of taking choices away from people.[5] A child sent to his room or a prisoner in a cell are deprived of options. The deprivation is supposedly in and of itself enough to make an offender think twice about repeating his offenses.[6] The central idea of punishment is this: Whether the offender lies to a friend or is a felon, he has taken resources from someone else solely for his own benefit. He has made his resource bank bigger while taking something out of that of the person he has harmed. A felon may take money without worrying about the theft's impact on his victim. An adulterer may take time or money or trust from his spouse. In any case, the harmed person becomes the object of the injurer's will. Harmed people are "done to" by another person and have no choices in the matter.

As I have said, the major resource taken from an unforgivably wounded person (or robbery victims or victims of assault) is choice. Injurers inflict their will upon other people. They make other people the objects of what they alone choose to do. They do not consult the wishes of the people they wound. Injurers load down the scale of resources on their side by taking things from others. Punishment supposedly balances the scale again.[7]

When someone is punished, he, like the person he offended, is also robbed of choice. A prisoner doing time or a child grounded for a week is deprived of the freedom to sift through available alternatives and make selections. People are punished so that they can feel what it is like to be the object of someone else's will. They become the object of someone else's choice. They, temporarily at least, lose free choice or will.

Supposedly, once a person has experienced this loss, he has learned his lesson. Choice is a terrible thing to be deprived of. And once a person has lost choice, he can have immense empathy for anyone else who has. (This is one reason that hostage taking fuels such passions. Everyone fears being the object of other people's choices.) Since everyone has been punished at some time, most people can empathize with a person robbed of his free will. So once the punishment is finished, we let each other go. We free each other because we can feel what each other feels.

Unforgivably wounded people who have a chance to punish their offenders do so in numerous ways. Whatever way they choose, they make their offenders temporary objects of their will. Mona, whose husband refused to suspend his affair, described the way she punished him for it.

> *I had changed, but he hadn't yet. But we were still living to-*
> *gether. I started saying all kinds of things. I mean, I really*
> *fought dirty verbally. Like while we were making love, I said,*
> *"You could give me herpes—you and your slut."*
>
> *My emotional response shook me. But it also shook him. He*
> *HEARD me. Before, when I said I was unhappy, he'd say, "I'm*
> *not. Your hormones are just screwy. This is all I want." I mean,*
> *to say THAT when I was so unhappy, being alone all of the time.*
> *He was omnipotent. He would not DO anything to make it a*
> *relationship. So I fought dirty until he heard me.*

To be the object of another person's verbal assaults is to have someone else's will imposed on your own. For Mona, verbal assaults helped her husband hear her and begin to put time and energy back into their marriage. For some people, verbal assaults have no effect. Other actions must be taken.

Jenny began to "do battle" to balance the scale with her abusive husband. As she described the methods she used to gain strength, her back stiffened. For a person horribly abused, she looked amazingly strong.

> *He was a bully, and bullies bully anyone who's frightened of*
> *them. Finally, I began to fight back. I hit him. This was a shock*
> *to him, I'll tell you. He had thought wives were slaves. "That's*

my dog; pet it. That's my car; polish it. That's my wife." For
many years, he couldn't understand that I didn't want to be a
shadow of him. He thought I should do everything like him. I
really wasn't a person. When I hit him, I started fighting back.

Of course, physical violence is not the best way to rob another
person of choice and to impose one's will upon another. In this
instance, the husband's shock at being someone else's victim, even
once, stopped him from continuing his abuse of her.

Verbal assaults and "battling" may be more uncommon than other
methods of punishment. Most people take more indirect action.
Withholding resources is the most common. Some wounded people
refuse to communicate with the person who hurt them, even when
the injurer is trying hard to reestablish communication. Some withhold sex. Some people tighten their hold over money. Others refuse
to allow their children to visit abusive parents. Whatever resource
is withheld, the withholding robs the injurer of choice. But for these
actions to be truly punitive, the offender needs to know why he is
being treated the way he is. Punishment does not work unless the
punished person is told the reasons he is being punished.[8] If reasons
are not understood, punishment is more like revenge, and the punished person is not sure what he must do to make things right.

Most people who successfully punish someone else not only inflict
their will on the person but also name the injury at the same time.
Just as a parent tells his child, "I'm sending you to your room because
you talked back to me," a wounded adult should punish with a clear
message behind the punishment. Withholding sex is not punishment.
Saying "I don't want to sleep with you for a while because you
destroyed my faith in your honesty and my idea of our future together" is effective punishment. It states what is withheld and why
it is being withheld. It also opens up the door for an apology and
for promises to be made. Punishment without condemnation will
never result in an apology because the person does not know why,
exactly, he is being treated in such a punitive way.[9]

One of the tricky things about punishment is that the punisher
needs to have a resource he can withhold or some strength he can

impose. For example, children are easy to punish because parents hold all of the family's resources. Parents can withhold either by grounding a teenager or refusing to give an allowance. Or they can use strength, like spanking or making a child write down an apology a hundred times. Society can use its strength to punish—through imprisonment, enforced restitution, or lengthy probation. But how can children punish adults who hold all the cards in their hands? The answer is that they usually cannot. During childhood, a person might run away from home or refuse to talk to his parents; but this is not punishment unless the parent knows the reasons for the child's behavior and is also deprived of a choice (e.g., the choice over whether to love or hug a child or have conversations with him). Most children do not have enough power to really punish parents until they become adults. By then, though, it may be too late. The parent may be too old to understand or even dead.

Since forgiving occurs (most of the time, anyhow) without the offender's participation (even if he is alive), punishment is often simply not possible. You have no way to strip your offender of choice if he is halfway across the country or involved in an entirely new life. When punishing is impossible for lack of resources, you will need to balance the scales using a different strategy.

POSSIBILITY THREE: LOADING THE SCALES

If you take a pound of apples from a balanced five-pound scale, the remaining four-pound side will be lighter; the scale is out of balance. To restore balance, a person must add a pound to replace the apples. The pound can be apples, oranges, or even stones.

When your resources are taken, you must purposely replace them by taking measures to load down resources on your side of the scale. Loading down the scale puts you back in a position of equality. It is accomplished, as punishment is, through taking purposeful action to regain advantage. It is important in the balancing phase to increase your own resources and choices on purpose so that it is your own accomplishments that give you a sense of personal power. If resources and choices come to you because of someone else's hard work and not your own, you may have more resources available, but they have not resulted from your active involvement in your healing.

Active involvement in the forgiving process enhances your self-esteem and makes the process move ahead more quickly. Jenny had fought back and punished her battering husband as much as she could; then she got a job.

> *I started back to work, and everyone liked me there. I had been smart in school, but I had had a huge inferiority complex. In fact, I had been in the highest standard in high school. At the job, I regained confidence in myself. I was really good at it.*

Forgivers I interviewed variously joined groups, started new relationships, took classes, found work, took on responsibilities, worked on political campaigns, and launched into numerous other activities. Each method dramatically increased the choices available to the wounded person. Through their activities, people made new friends, gained access to financial resources, and reacquainted themselves with their own strengths. Roseanne, the woman whose husband engaged in fraudulent business practices and subsequently lost everything the couple owned, including their home, remembered who she had been before the marriage and applied her skills to a new job in a nursing home.

> *I had always been outgoing. Always able to get along with all sorts of people. In school, I had been elected to all kinds of things. I managed the school canteen and was a monitor on the playground—that kind of stuff. So I decided to try to work at this nursing home and found out again that people really liked me.*

Possibly because paradox is a powerful phenomenon, the people I interviewed who seemed the strongest and most at peace were those who used their own injuries to enhance their resources. If you create a gift for yourself out of your own tragedy, you might create one of the most powerful psychological paradoxes of all.

Nancy, who was still in the throes of grief after her son poisoned himself, began to use the loss to help other people.

> *I got involved with a group called "Compassionate Friends"—a support group for parents who have lost their children. It's all composed of bereaved parents. I had been working at the cemetery one day, and a young woman came out to water a vase for her little boy's grave and started to cry. And like all of us do when we cry, she started to apologize. I just put my arms around her and said, "You don't have to cry, 'cause I know how you feel." Then she told me that she was getting involved with a group that was based in Illinois. I said, "Well, let me know." About a year later, a pamphlet to do with the Compassionate Friends appeared on my desk with her name on it, and I ended up becoming chapter leader of a group that met in town. I gained a great deal from that.*
>
> *One of the things I realized was I had never forgiven my husband because I didn't know that men and women grieved differently. I discovered from a mutual friend that he had gone over to their home and cried to them after our son had died, and I never knew it. So I asked him to forgive me for not understanding that his grief, while it wasn't the same as mine, was nonetheless real and painful for him to deal with. I asked him to forgive me for my feelings.*

This is how people transcend their wounds. Divorced people in pain generated new groups for other divorced people in pain. Other wounded people began other kinds of groups. When forgivers make their pain work to the benefit of others, they become stronger.

Many great people have used their suffering to make other people's lives better. Story after story has emerged from prisoners of war and survivors of the Holocaust who were able to turn their horrors into strengths. Similarly, people who survive intimate injuries are able to turn those injuries into good. Each of us can help another person (or many other people) if we use our experiences to ease the difficulties of others. When you discover that you must balance the scale with your injurer through loading your side down with additional resources, the good you create from using the injury is an active, purposeful pursuit. It is bold and gutsy. To take action means to move beyond self-absorption or self-pity and look to others who may need you.

You can load the scales by adding accomplishment to the depleted side. Or you can weigh down the scale by deriving new advantages from the injury itself. Whichever way it is done, you are no longer at the mercy of someone else's will, but instead create your own opportunities. The creation of opportunity takes work, but the pay-offs in self-esteem and restored balance are enormous.

POSSIBILITY FOUR: MIRRORING THE INJURY, OR MOCK PUNISHMENT

When a wounded person is powerless to punish or too young to load the scale to his advantage, there is a fourth method often used—unconsciously—to balance the scale. The technique, called mirroring the injury, must be mentioned because it happens to injured people fairly often, and it can be very self-destructive. Mirroring does not increase choices available to the injured person, as loading does, *or* impose the harmed person's will onto the harmer, as punishing does. Instead, the wounded person repeats his own injury; only this time he becomes the harmer.

People who are abandoned abandon others. People who were lied to lie to others. The wounded, in other words, wound. While this may seem to be an illogical way of balancing the scales, it really is not. If a person becomes as "bad" as his injurer, the "badness" scale is balanced. Then the wounded person can understand the injurer better and identify with him and with his motives. This makes it easier to forgive because he can empathize with the one who hurt him.

Mirroring the injury is a common phenomenon of people who were unforgivably wounded as children. A common example is the abused child who grows up to abuse his own children. Once he has done this, he can empathize with his own abusive parents.

Mirroring, however, is also used by adults wounded by other adults. Janet, whose husband had affairs with his high school students, put it this way:

> *I had affairs, too. It was just great. I felt free and alive again, so I started understanding why he did it. It had nothing to do with me, really. It had to do with something about himself that he was unhappy with. I couldn't hold him responsible for being unhappy with himself any more than I could hold myself to blame for my own unhappiness.*

Mirroring, like other methods of balancing the scale, evens up power differentials and allows the harmed person to "get inside the mind" of his injurer. Once people have engaged in behavior similar to the behavior that hurt them, they can finally understand that anyone can do harm, even themselves. Anyone can be harmed, too. In a way, mirroring is an unconscious effort to equalize blame so that compassion for the injurer overtakes hatred for him. Mirroring also allows a person to experience the power that was used against him.

Since mirroring is ordinarily not a conscious procedure—that is, since the mirroring person may not understand why he behaves the way he does—it is less effective than other methods of balancing. Balancing is purposeful and active. Mirroring the injury is not. Thus, if a wounded person wounds back, it is better for him to understand that there are more positive ways to retrieve power and self-esteem.

In a sense, mirroring the injury is like war. War is, after all, a common way to bring resources back into balance. The ebb and flow of one army—advance, attack, retreat, defend—is countered by the advance, attack, retreat, and defend of the other army. Finally, the resulting carnage blurs right and wrong. All soldiers are injured; all are injurers. Injured and injurers become one and the same.

When a wounded person wounds others continually, he may finally be able to empathize with and understand the one who wounded him, but the damage left behind as a result is not worth it. No one wins; everyone loses. Even if forgiveness flows from knowing oneself as a person capable of hurting others, forgiveness has come with a very high price tag. There are better ways.

One final method for balancing the scale can be used when no other way is available. The method is called *mock punishment*.

Mock punishment, like punishment in general, consists of reminding the offender of the rules he broke, condemning him for it, and finally making him the object of one's will for a little while. The difference between punishment and mock punishment is that in punishment the action is taken against the offender; in mock punishment, it is taken against some substitute offender. There is a substitute for the offender because he is no longer available to be punished. (He may be dead or live far away.)

Several forms of mock punishment are common when wounded people balance the scale. The most ordinary are quiet, private undertakings. Some people, however, engage in more aggressive behavior.

Among the private methods of mock punishment is the condemnation letter. Mary Ann, whose alcoholic father hurt her in many ways both as a child and as an adult, explained how she wrote letters to him even though she never sent them.

> *My own process was to go through an accusing phase, then to listen to the person I'm accusing. I mean really listen. Well, the process is totally MY process. No one else has to be there. First, I would write down everything he did. I would accuse him. I had tried to excuse him before, you know, find rationales, but that didn't work. It was always in the back of my mind. The hate didn't go away. So I realized I needed to accept the hate first before I could move on. Once I allowed myself to be in a rage, it was easy. You don't have to know why something happens. First you just have to accept your feelings.*
>
> *So I accused. Then I listened. Sometimes I wrote letters back. When I did that, I could understand his humanness, too.*

Writing accusations to substitute offenders can be an extremely effective method of mock punishment. So can telling a friend or therapist what you might want to say to the harmer if he were present. Imagination plays an important part in mock punishment. One forgiver described how she, through her vivid imagination, buried her horribly abusive mother.

> *I shut the drapes and went into the living room, and I pretended I was digging a grave in the living-room carpet. This must have taken all day. I lost track of time. And I wanted to get it done before my husband got home.*
>
> *So then I kicked her into the grave and was saying things like "You ruined my life. You make me afraid of everything." Stuff like that. Then I poured dirt on her—even in her mouth. And I covered her eyes up—then her face—with dirt. I just screamed and screamed. And cried. It went on for hours. I hoped no one heard.*
>
> *Then—it was over. I've never felt hate again.*

People harmed as children may have no resources with which to fight back. Like this forgiver, they may have to wait until they are adults to punish their injurer. As aggressive as a mock burial sounds, it may be much healthier than repeating the injury over and over with other unsuspecting people as victims of a wounded child. Punishment is not wrong. Violence is. Punishment is a person's and a society's way to restore balance and to prepare people for reacceptance. Society's reacceptance is restored privileges and a clean slate for the criminal. A person's reacceptance is forgiveness and a powerful heart.

Summary

The fourth phase of forgiving, balancing the scales, is filled with activity. It changes people from objects of other people's choices to people who create their own choices. Since forgiveness can be accomplished only if you feel strong enough, it is best to think of balancing the scales as a time when muscles are redeveloped or depleted stockpiles of goods are replenished.

It may seem odd to consider intimate relationships as transactions in which resources are finely balanced in a way that pleases both parties. But that is what relationships really are. When one person unforgivably harms someone who is delicately in balance with him, it is like the slapstick routine in which one character jumps on the end of a catapult and launches his unsuspecting victim like a rocket ship to sure injury. When all the weight falls on the offender's side of the balanced scale, new weight must be added to the empty side. This takes work, but work on one's own behalf is the best kind a wounded person can do. In fact, as sad as it may seem, no one else *can* do the work that restores power to a wounded person. It takes guts and humor and, above all, resolve that forgiveness can and will come.

As in all of the previous phases of forgiving, it's crucial not to get stuck balancing the scale, punishing endlessly, or mirroring self-destructively. Balancing resources (like claiming or figuring out who is to blame) is a phase—no more.

For people who have tried all the methods of balancing the scales—punishing, loading, mock punishment—but nothing seems to be enough, it is time to move forward anyhow. No punishment will restore the relationship to its original state. No resources will seem equal to the ones that the injurer took. Nothing will stop the harbored anger or unremitting hatred. There is nothing left but to move forward to the final action of forgiving: choosing to forgive. Whether you feel strong and in full command of your resources or you've made another person submit to your will and have punished him or you still feel weak and angry, the next move is to choose to forgive. It is simply easier to make that choice if you feel back on top of things.

CHAPTER **8**

Phase Five: Choosing to Forgive

To forgive, or not to forgive: That is the choice.

NANCY

That's how I felt about my son's death—that if I went on hating that woman and I didn't forgive her, I would end up having that kind of attitude toward everything I touched, including me. And so I felt I had a choice to make. Either I went ahead and said, okay, it doesn't mean that I agree with what she did, but I have to find it in my heart to forgive her. Because I don't want to have all that hatred pointed back at me. And that's what I think it does.

It's like an abscess inside you that just grows and grows. And then it affects all the other things that you touch. I discovered for me that the way I love or hate is so consuming I cannot do both things at once.

It seemed to me that loving was a lot nicer and happier and

more positive. And I know that is what my son would have
preferred. And I wanted to love my daughter and the man I
was married to.

These were Nancy's words as she described the choice she had to
make to forgive the woman who seduced her son. She knew her life
would never be the same after his death. She had hated and blamed
and confronted the young woman. She had become active in helping
other bereaved parents. She had made new friends. She had exhausted
her methods for punishing the woman. She had become as strong
as she was able to be. The only thing left for her was the choice to
forgive or not to forgive. Nancy chose to forgive; and what is most
obvious in her story, and all stories of true forgiveness, is that she
finally forgave for the sake of her own well-being, not for the well-
being of the one who hurt her. Forgiveness comes when it is the
only obstacle to freedom left.

What Nancy's story makes clear is that while some phases of forgiving are more emotional, the final phases are rational. Choosing
to forgive is guided by, and generated from, clearheaded thinking.
It springs, really, from self-preservation.

Self-preservation is the instinct that keeps us and other animals
alive. It is a barrier between life and death because it warns people
to stay clear of harm that might destroy them. It is only wise to
choose courses of action that preserve one's being. That is what the
forgiver does.

An unforgivable injury that has festered and grown is like a worm
crawling into an apple. It can take hold of your core and damage
the heart permanently. Unforgivable injuries break dreams and assault beliefs; but if they are allowed to damage your core, you have
let someone else not only destroy your dreams but destroy *you*. That
is too high a price to pay for anything. It is one thing to have your
heart broken; it is quite another to have it poisoned. Broken hearts
repair. Poisoned hearts shrivel and die. If a worm is poisoning your
heart, have it removed. If nonforgiveness is poisoning your heart,
then choose to eliminate it.

What does the choice to forgive really mean? It means you no longer expect that the person who injured you owes you anything. It means that you set the injurer free. It means that you don't look back. You no longer look at why the injury happened; you now look at what you will do and who you will be in the future.

Choosing to forgive, phase five, is a turning point—actually a pivotal point—in a person's life. Once the choice is made, a brand-new life lies ahead. That is the main reason that choosing to forgive is scary. Nothing is the same, at least where the injurer is concerned, once the choice is made.

Tasks of Choosing to Forgive

As in all the phases of forgiving, there are barriers to break through and tasks to be accomplished. Some of the barriers are fairly formidable, but once they are recognized, they can be overcome. The three tasks to be accomplished are as follows:

1. Making the choice to release the injurer from debt
2. Making the choice to cut the bonds that still hold you to the injurer
3. Making the choice to look ahead, not back

With choice comes responsibilities; but with choice there is also freedom.

TASK 1: CHOOSING TO EXPECT THAT NO DEBT BE REPAID

Choosing to forgive is like any other choice. Anytime you choose one thing, you lose another. So if you choose to expect no further payments from your injurer and to stop punishing, what could you possibly lose? The answer is "plenty."

Probably the biggest loss faced when you require that no more debt be paid is the sense of self-righteousness that has come from being so harmed. Mary Ann described her resistance to abandoning her moral high ground with this explanation:

> *I hung on to pain before. You know, it feels good in a sick sort of way—"Fuck you." When you do that, you're building yourself up to stay in that place. It's in a false way, though. If I can keep you in a bad place, then that makes me look pretty good. So I knew I couldn't start forgiving until I got sober. It's a very painful thing to go through. But living is a rational process; it's a choice, a definite responsibility. And as long as the rational mind is suppressed, like with alcohol, it's impossible. I said to myself, "If I want to like myself and to feel good with other people, I need to do that." I'm responsible for my well-being. I can choose not to go through the process and hurt and be in pain, but what good would that do? So I had to give all that up.*

Self-righteousness does not mean arrogance. It means that when a person finally decides that she was wronged by someone else, she gains strength. To reject that conclusion might seem like losing strength again. Self-righteousness in the choosing phase has nothing to do with who was right and who was wrong. It has nothing to do with weakness. To release another from debt does not mean that they were right all along and that you were wrong. It only means that even though you were right and they hurt you, you do not want them to pay you back. Throughout the other phases of forgiving, an injured person should have become so strong that she does not *need* anything from the injurer. Punishment and loading the scales have balanced the relationship out. No redistribution of goods is required to balance the amount of resources held by the injured and the injurer. To require no payment from the offender does not imply that blame be put aside. Instead, it requires that no further exchanges between injured and injurer are necessary. Neither owes the other a thing.

Every choice brings with it not only a loss but also a new set of responsibilities. When you forgive someone, you say to yourself, "The person who hurt me is no longer responsible for the way my life will go. I am responsible now." When you choose to want nothing from your injurer, you abandon the idea of making that person responsible for anything in your future. To take on responsibility for one's life is tough. Many of us would like to have someone else around to blame for our bad fortunes. When we choose to expect no repayments, though, we give up the luxury of having the injurer around to blame for our attitudes or our pain. Pain and attitudes become the sole property of the wounded, who alone will decide what to do with them.

Choosing to forgive, in other words, increases personal responsibilities. It particularly influences who the wounded person believes responsible for her well-being in the future. Mona, whose husband refused to go with her to therapy and then attributed her unhappiness to hormone imbalance, recognized that when she chose to forgive, she became reliant on herself for her own future happiness.

> *Happy? Unhappy? It's all in me. My expectations have changed. I wouldn't be amazed by anything. I think I can anticipate anything. I've learned that I'm physically, emotionally, and psychologically a separate entity. It all comes from within me. Reality is not happiness; it is a state. And what you do in that state determines the happiness factor.*

Not only are your responsibilities to yourself altered when you choose to expunge any debts; your responsibilities to others are also altered. These responsibilities were some of the last changes that Joan (who played the joke on herself when her comment about divorce actually resulted in it) acknowledged in her process of forgiving.

> *To harbor anger, you lose a lot of responsibility. Anger is a great excuse not to visit a forgetful old person or drive across town to do a favor. If you forgive, you're right back in the human race as a responsible person. Forgiving has nothing to do with trust. It means you have to take risks again. You are vulnerable again. By forgiving my ex, I had to allow the kids to have a stepmother.*

I had to allow them to see him, maybe even get them over to his house. Anger allows you not to have to meet obligations—buying gifts, doing favors. That's why forgiving is so hard. You have to get back in it again.

To do away with a debt is to forsake any remaining idea that the injurer has resources that you want. Even if the injurer is rich, happily remarried, or flying around the world, when you choose to forgive, in your *heart*, you want nothing from the person who hurt you— not an apology, a promise, a loan, or a plane trip. You are strong within yourself. You need nothing from your injurer and wish no harm. You are even.

These things you choose. They do not just happen. But while choice brings responsibilities, the new freedom in your life is well worth it.

Task Two: Setting the Injurer Free

There is a bond between injured and injurer. In unforgivable wounds, the bond is love turned to grief and loss turned to hate. A final bond that ties two people driven apart by the unforgivable is the thread of hope that the relationship can be restored as it once was. It cannot. As Joan said, "Forgiveness is a closure. It closes a door and releases you to start fresh."

Any forgiveness closes a door. The door you have left open may be the vain hope that an abusive parent will finally provide the unconditional love that you were deprived of as a child. Or you may secretly believe that an old lover will leave her current partner and return to you, even after she has been gone for years.

In a way, the two people in an intimate injury are defined by each other. There cannot be a victim without a perpetrator or a captive without a captor. Similarly, there can be no unforgivably wounded person without an injurer. So, to set the injurer free is to set the injured free. If one is no longer an injurer, the other can no longer think of herself as "injured."

Imagine the relationship between zookeeper and caged zoo animal.

One day, the zookeeper, after caring for a great lioness for many years, decides to open the cage door and free her. The door swings open, the lioness looks out. She takes a giant leap toward freedom and bounds across the grass and over the fence. Both kept and keeper no longer exist in relation to each other. The bond is broken. To say "I forgive you" accomplishes this same end. The injurer is free, no longer an injurer. And the injured is free, no longer the injured. Even the forgiver who struggles alone, without a physically present injurer, feels the same result. The words "I forgive you," uttered in a therapist's office or in a living room at night, still signal—even without the injurer's presence—the breaking of a bond, the end of something powerful and important.

The lioness in the parable may choose to return to her cage; perhaps she doesn't know where else to sleep. Her return does not again make her a captive, nor does it make the zookeeper a captor. The lioness has chosen the familiar; the zookeeper has chosen to allow her that option. Regardless, their relationship is permanently changed.

People who forgive their spouses and stay with them, friends who reaffirm their bonds, or parents and children who free each other know that things will always be different. The relationships are *not* restored. They may be reaffirmed but not restored.

Janet, who stayed with her husband rather than divorce him after his affair, put it this way:

> *Things will never be the same. They're better. I see him now as a real person. You know, he represented some person I manufactured in my head. As it turns out, he's not a lot like what I thought I married. I'm probably not, either. You can go out and look for a new manufactured thing or stick with what you had. I concluded the early passion is the best it's going to get. It just happened, that's all. It's just different. You know, passion that lasts forever doesn't exist. You can't sustain it. There are moments, moments in time. The real world, though, is pretty pragmatic; it's pretty functional. I haven't given up those moments, but we've just changed.*

It is a very brave act to say, "I choose to forgive you. You are free." Just as cutting a balloon from a string allows it to rise into the clouds, forgiving no longer holds the injurer in check. There will be memories and pictures in an album and a history that is valid. Forgiving does not erase validity. Just because you let someone go does not mean the relationship was not at one time meaningful. Forgiveness validates the memory of a relationship because it acknowledges that there was caring, then pain, then freeing the self to go on with what remains of life ahead.

People, in general, do not like to sever bonds. We do not do it well. In fact, though, once a bond has been severed by an injurer, the only way the injured person can also sever it is to forgive. In a way, saying "I forgive you" is quite similar in its effect to the original injury. Saying "I forgive you" is done with benefiting oneself as its goal. It severs a once-moral relationship, and it is the start of a new life for the wounded person. Unlike the acts of the unforgivable injurer, though, saying "I forgive you" is not vicious or a violation of a moral contract. It does not enhance one person's position while it takes something from someone else. It is the gift of freedom given by the forgiver to herself and to the one who harmed her. Neither owes the other, and both are free.

Besides assuming new responsibilities and severing the thread between people, there is one more barrier to forgiving—this one central to the reason many people have such a hard time freeing their harmer.

Once an unforgivable injury occurs, no matter how awful it is, it does generate some positive side effects. In the early phases, people may find out new things about themselves as they stumble through their daily lives of pain. They may make friends and find support from their families. They may like the new values they recognize in themselves. In the later, active phases of forgiveness, the harmed may even generate positive supports for other people who hurt or need help. If these activities provide new strengths for the wounded, those strengths will be piled up higher and higher upon themselves as the wounded heals. If, on the other hand, the activities become a central point of the harmed person's emerging new identity, choosing to forgive can become almost too difficult to accomplish. It means that very difficult losses will follow.

If an injured person has become used to, and attached to, an identity that is tied closely to the injury, she will probably think of herself in terms of a label. Some of them might be "battered wife" or "incest victim" or "child of an alcoholic." These labels are powerful sources of identity for many people. They pigeonhole people according to the way they were hurt. Each label has generated specialists. There are therapists, for example, who specialize in working with incest victims and treatment groups for battered women. For people who have become attached to other group members or to their therapists, the paradox is that if they let go of their labels, they will sooner or later have no need for those who have helped them. They will have to let them go, too.

Most people are quite ready to lose these labels and move ahead. For some people, though, feeling special, even if the feeling is derived from a terrible wound, may be their first experience in thinking of themselves as unique in any way. When someone chooses to set her harmer free by cutting the cord of small hope between them, the forgiver no longer defines anything about herself in reference to her injurer. A forgiver defines herself; and the definition is absent of references to being wounded or to being a victim. A person who succeeds in forgiving wants nothing from her injurer—not even a label.

Every setting free of a person you have loved, even if it is only a "minor" setting free, carries with it a mourning. When people set others free, their roles change. This is the reason parents cry at their children's weddings, even when they are happy. The role between parents and their married child is different from the one they have had with the single child. Now the new spouse will step in and take over some of the functions of the parent. When children leave home and their parents have, for the first time, set them free, there is mourning. There is also great happiness, but setting anything free, even a bird from a cage to take wing, can bring a lump to the throat. To forgive is to let go of past dreams and "could have been"s. What might have been will not be. Life will go on, but it will be different from your previous expectations. Mourning the passing of a dream is positive. Not forgiving for fear of mourning can paralyze and poison you.

Fear of a loss of the validity of one's past, fear of new responsibilities, fear of having no special identity, and fear of mourning can each stand in the way of saying "I forgive you." So some of the tasks of choosing to forgive become clearer when you recognize such fears as the final obstacle to forgiving and decide to do something about them.

Saying "I forgive you" when you are ready is a powerful action. It can be a moment when freedom explodes.

You can say it aloud to the one who hurt you, to a picture in an album, or to a chair you pretend is that person. Because of the fears associated with the words, though, saying it may need some additional explanation, particularly if you are not able to address your injurer directly.

If any of the four fears prevents the final choice to forgive, you may want to practice what you will, or would like to, say to your injurer. Here are four choices, each of which can affirm the final choice to set the harmer free.

1. "I forgive you. Our relationship was valid and meaningful. Now we'll both move forward."
2. "I forgive you. I am ready to take on any new responsibilities that come to me because I have made this choice."
3. "I forgive you. I am still a special person and maybe even more special because I can forgive. I don't need a label to identify me."
4. "I forgive you. And I know I will mourn my loss of you."

Saying these sentences aloud can help you hear your own fears expressed. If you are stuck at the point of setting your injurer free, verbalizing your losses along with your new freedoms might push you over the hump. To become disabled just barely short of the goal of forgiving is unhappy business. To come so far in the process and

not complete it can paralyze you psychologically for many years—
or forever.

TASK THREE: LOOKING AHEAD

There is a Joan Baez song whose lyrics read:

> It is said to never look back . . .
> To shadows you left on the track . . .
> Gather your roses and run
> The long way around.
>
> And if the time should ever be right, my love . . .
> I'll come to you in the night, my love . . .
> But now there is only the sorrow.
> Parting is near, Parting is here.
> Parting is here, Parting is here.

When you have parted from your injurer, you look forward, not
back. This is not to say you don't recall things in the past. You just
choose not to dwell there. Like the god Janus, you keep an eye on
the past to know where you have come from and what road has
brought you here. The other eye looks ahead at the unknown with
a clear and steady gaze.

The difference between the looking forward of the Baez lyrics and
that of the forgiver is that letting go may bring a fleeting sorrow,
but it is soon over. Anticipation and a newly felt freedom replace
any lingering sorrow.

I asked Janet what she would tell someone who couldn't forgive.
She responded with a smile:

> *Forgiveness is a virtue, I think. Anger brings you nothing. No*
> *sleep; no smiling. Then it spurts out into other areas. . . . God*
> *doesn't want you to be miserable—mentally or physically. If you*
> *are harboring anger or wanting revenge, you are not doing God's*
> *will for you. You're not allowing yourself to be the person God*
> *wants you to be. Forgiveness is a fantastic way to live. It releases*

you from so much. You can never again be so angry. Never as intense. Never for so long. I think it's one of the most important things to be able to do. It's accepting the fact that no one is perfect.

The choice to forgive is an invitation to freedom. It is the one chance you may actually have to choose to start your life over again, fresh and with a clean slate.

An Invitation to Freedom

I asked forgivers what they would say to someone who was struggling to forgive. Here are some of their responses:

You can afford to treat everyone as though they have a broken heart, because usually they do. And they do. It may not be apparent. Very often it's the person who laughs the most or jokes the most who is broken inside. Everyone is hurting from something, and once you realize that, you can become more compassionate in your attitude toward them. I try to remember that everyone is trying to be the best person they can be at that particular time. And if they don't meet my expectations, that isn't really their fault. Most of the time, they don't even know what my expectations are.

If you ask me to put it all in one sentence, I'd say forgiveness is like a freedom. Like a toothache, when they take it out, that ache is gone. You don't think about THAT one anymore. It's like a freeing—a cleansing within yourself.

It is like a moment, a lifting. When I put myself in someone else's shoes, I could understand. Then I could let go. I think forgiveness is good mental health.

I made a distinction between forgiving in the head and forgiving in the heart. To not forgive in your heart destroys your health and your heart. People should know, though, that it is hurdle after hurdle.

I wouldn't want my husband back on a silver platter, but I've forgiven him. Forgiving had not so much to do with him or me. It's the ability to be free and to live one's own life.

In our business, we have a term: "normalization." Return to normal. When I think of defining forgiveness, I have to think of the process I've gone through. Accepting things for what they are, what has gone on. Then just say, "Forget it," and get on with it. It's happened. That's reality. Let's get on with it.

You just don't dwell on things anymore. It's not the right heart condition to have. Forgiving is loving another person, or at least trying to. Maybe they had some problems they couldn't cope with. But you don't have to hang around with them. You might be capitalizing on their weakness if you did that.

I realized that forgiveness was an act of will, not of feelings. I had thought it was about feeling. And I knew I could never feel loving about him. But when I realized it was intellectual, it was such a relief. I can solve anything intellectually. So it was like a freeing that had been happening slowly. I was able to recognize that I had loved him in the beginning. But I had denied it.

When I forgave him, I understood that I had not been the cause of anything. The only thing I had been the cause of was my own emotions. Because I forgave him, it was as if I forgave myself because I thought I was a bad person all the time. Never him.

Not to forgive means not being the person you want to be. Not forgiving can do terrible things to a person. It changes you.

Forgiveness is having compassion, but I don't want to retrace my steps.

By harboring angry and bad thoughts about anybody, you make yourself sick. You have to throw it out.

To forgive, you have to feel good about yourself and be a strong person. There has to be a little good in every person. No one can be all bad.

You forgive the whole person, not just the act. The big thing is not to build up a wall. If you don't forgive, it changes you. You're not you. You're not good, not healthy, not happy. You stagnate. It's not worth it to hold on to grudges. I don't want to waste time.

You have to be able to accept the act and fully understand it. Then you should be able to talk about it, not push it under the rug. Then after you're rid of the anger and despair and feel good about yourself again (I mean, for a while I didn't feel good about myself), once you have your feelings intact, you can finally forgive. The actual forgiveness comes after the hurt goes away.

Forgiveness should be something you want to do. Some people can hold grudges and go on. They're perfectly happy with things unstraightened. I can't live like that. If you honestly want to forgive someone, do it. Don't be afraid they'll laugh at you. They're probably hurting as much as you are. Forgiving makes you feel cleaner, easier. It's almost like taking a bath.

I think that forgiving, to me, is realizing that hate and anger and those feelings do not hurt the person you're directing them at, but they hurt you. And just coming to a rational decision that I've got to do good things for me instead of bad things for me.

Forgiveness means to write a person off. Never let them close again. Never trust them again. It is not healing or reconciliation;

it's just forgetting it and not giving it the opportunity to happen again.

Forgiveness begins a whole new relationship. You don't want to build on a crumbled relationship. Forgiveness is erasing whatever the situation or circumstances were at the time you felt you couldn't forgive. It becomes null and void. It doesn't exist. It never existed.

If people can find within themselves any little bit that would help them forgive someone versus holding on to it, pursue it, because it's one of the most beautiful experiences a person can have.

To really know, within yourself, that you have actually forgiven that person—it's something you read about, but you can't imagine how it would affect you. It can only affect you in a beautiful way.

Forgiving is integrating whatever it is you're dealing with into your whole life, your whole person. So you'll get the perspective right. If you do that, you can move on. Not to forgive is to be stuck.

At some point in time, you just have to let go of negative feelings for your own sanity. If you don't want to do it for the other person's sake, do it for your own.

Some things another person does to you can never be made up for. And what would be the point, even if you could get even? How even can you really get? You make a conscious decision. Then you can take it one step further and let the person know you've forgiven them. You can take that burden away from them. Not including the person who hurt you is like a job half-done. You give a gift; someone has to receive it.

Forgiving is being able to be at peace with yourself. I don't want to restore the relationship; I didn't even like it before this all happened.

Tell people if they want to survive, you don't think of how many years it's going to last. You think of tomorrow. And you've got to realize happiness is not a big, bulky package tied up with a bow. Happiness, even in the worst situations, is there because children smile; you talk to your neighbor; a kiss from a baby; a flower or a beer or a boat; or a cobweb in the morning sun. These are the things that you look at, and they can sustain your soul, I suppose. They give you energy to battle what you've got to battle for.

You've got to be like an alcoholic and take one day at a time and hope it will be better. Perhaps have a plan for the future to work for. It might be only a dream, but even if it's only a dream, it gives you a reason to keep going and face up to life and to accept the beauty around you and restore yourself.

CHAPTER **9**

Phase Six: The Emergence of a New Self

> If something devastates your life, a complete reorganization begins. I needed a whole new philosophy about people.
>
> JANET

Buck and Amanda Jones and their only son, Ted, were integral members of their small community. Buck taught history and gym; Amanda taught fourth grade. The Joneses were active in nearly everything in the community that involved children—4H, Scouts, church youth fellowship, band, and any special cause for kids that called for volunteers. Ted was an outstanding student, class president, and football player. He was to graduate in the spring.

The Jones household was warm and inviting. Teenagers loved to go there, including a troubled boy named Martin. Martin's father had been in and out of trouble with the law for years, and Martin himself had gotten into a few scrapes. They were minor, but the Joneses wanted to extend themselves to Martin and to help him out if they could. They became Martin's second parents.

One fall weekend, the Joneses' house had been filled with teenagers and the smell and sounds of popcorn and music. By late in the afternoon, most of the kids had gone home to supper, and the Joneses had returned to normal. A few boys still lingered. Martin was one of them.

For some reason the Joneses never understood, the boys decided to load their rifles and go out into the field to target shoot. (Hunting season was over, so it was a chore to get the guns out.) In a light mist, four boys headed out the door with their guns and took off in different directions. When Ted appeared over a small knoll, Martin fired. The bullet hit him in the head. He died instantly.

The Joneses struggled to forgive for years. They could blame Martin, but nothing could return their loss. Of course, nothing ever did. Slowly, though, the couple returned to volunteer work and community activity. One day, out of the blue, an unusual opportunity was presented them. A friend in the community knew of a tiny baby in another state that needed adoptive parents. The friend thought he could arrange for the Joneses to adopt little Jason. At nearly fifty, Buck and Amanda became parents again. Their numbness began to give way to love.

Other things had given way also. The Joneses had forgiven Martin, but over the forgiving process, they had replaced almost every significant belief they had once held. They gave up the church. They no longer believed in the concept of fairness. And they no longer equated their good deeds with rewards to follow. Everything they had believed had changed. They were different people.

A person who succeeds in forgiving an unforgivable injury has gone through a conversion, or more accurately, conversions. He has been forced to accept that his core beliefs have failed him and to acknowledge that new beliefs will, in all likelihood, be erected in their place.

The series of miniconversions a forgiver goes through finally culminate in the forging of a new person who has a transformed outlook on his world. In a paradoxical way, unforgivable injuries present you with one of life's opportunities to change fundamentally. The experience of being wounded may force you against your will to alter your dreams, myths, and expectations of life; but where else can you experience a confrontation so rare? To really be able to transform one's essential beliefs is a chance of a lifetime. To do it well is an art.

Most people, like it or not, believe what they have always believed. Ideas about criminals, poverty, deserving and undeserving victims, God, rich people, love, felons, religion, bad luck—on and on—take seed early in life and finally become rooted as the foundation of your conceptualization of your world. Information that enters your perceptual field ordinarily is filtered, then synthesized, through your beliefs until it fits nicely into your long-established view of the world. Someone who considers all believers in UFOs, for instance, to be eccentric dreamers probably concludes that the alien he sees standing next to a spaceship in his backyard is the next-door neighbor kid dressed in a space suit. This fits his belief. A true believer in alien visitors, by comparison, might think a distant Frisbee obscured in the sunlight is a flying saucer from one of Jupiter's moons. People see what they believe. Over time, they become stuck in their beliefs about life and each other. Everything fits nicely together in a comfortable but unchanging package.

No one *wants* the security of his beliefs to be tampered with, of course, especially when the tampering is against his will and results in terrible pain. Once beliefs or myths are shattered, though, an opportunity awaits. It is like a moment when a disbeliever confronts an alien from outer space and *knows* it is an alien from outer space; he has been given a chance to restructure his very basic beliefs about life itself. Who controls things? How much power do we really have? Do some people deserve to be hurt, while others do not? The unharmed never have to face such serious challenges to their assumptions. Forgivers do; and through the process of forgiving, they find and create new answers that, in a way, make them new people. While most people would not wish this upon themselves, it is one of life's ways of giving people a second chance. To be wounded, in this strange way, is to be given a gift.

The final phase of forgiving is called the *emergence of a new self.* It is in this phase that the word "forgiving" begins to make sense. "For" and "giving" can be interpreted to mean that a wound is for giving. A wound gives you a chance to end one thing and begin something else. It is the gift of a new beginning. At the end of a long journey, a traveler might unpack his suitcase, do the laundry, read the mail, and get mentally prepared to go back to work. Or he might pack his bags and set off on another trip the next day. The point is, life begins again. For the forgiver, life begins again as well.

People who forgive sever themselves from the past and look to the future. In the emergence of a new self, the person who has gone through major conversions in his beliefs about very central things in his life (like other travelers) ends his journey, unpacks his figurative bags, and gets life back to normal. Whatever he chooses to do, it will be a time when his new beliefs gathered along the journey to forgiveness are consolidated and tested. Regardless, so many fundamental changes have happened, he will not go back and retrace his steps. It is one of life's paradoxical gifts that the end of the process of forgiving is a second chance. If nothing can ever be the same, this time around it can be even better.

The Miniconversions on the Journey to Forgiveness

People who have forgiven have gone through at least eight "miniconversions." A forgiver converts

1. From a person who does not understand the harm done to him to someone who incorporates his injury to one who no longer considers himself to be injured.
2. From a person who blames himself to someone who blames another to one who blames no one.
3. From a person who does not want to change to someone who accepts that he must change to one who directs the course of his change.
4. From a person who wants the present to return to the past to

someone who hangs on to the present to one who looks only to the future.

5. From a person who is acted upon to someone who cannot act to one who acts on the things he knows he can act on.
6. From a person who trusts to someone who does not trust to one who may choose to trust if he wants.
7. From a person who loves to someone who hates to someone who either loves in a different way or is indifferent to the injurer.
8. From a person who feels equal in power or resources to someone who feels depleted of resources to one who feels equal again.

These conversions happen when people stop off at the first five phases of forgiving. Forgivers begin to change their perceptions, their behavior, their values, and their expectations. But the major transformation of forgiveness is more basic: It is the transformation in the way a person sees the fundamentals of life. At the end of the forgiving process, the miniconversions come together and converge at a point. It is at this point that the wounded person is transformed because his beliefs in the fundamentals of life are transformed.

The Transformation of Forgiveness

Forgiving propels people toward the creation of a new set of personal beliefs. Once the beliefs you had about your life have been altered, new ones must take their place. Throughout the whole forgiving process and its conversions, your individual beliefs have changed little by little. By individual beliefs, I mean your beliefs, for instance, about harm or control have changed independently of one another. Independently also, your ideas about yourself and other people and spiritual matters have undergone shifts. But while independent beliefs have shifted, forgiveness is not final for people until the independent beliefs fit harmoniously together once again. Until that time, people experience distress.

According to psychologists, human nature strives to maintain consistency among behaviors, values, and attitudes. When inconsistency occurs, people experience a form of distress called cognitive dissonance.[1]

Cognitive dissonance might have happened to you in this way: Before the injury, you believed you were a worthy person and God looked after you. After the injury, you were no longer sure how worthy you were because you believed God would not have allowed such a painful experience to happen if you had been. One belief must have been wrong—the belief that you were worthy or that God looked after you. When two beliefs like this collide, people undergo cognitive dissonance. Nothing fits together in any sensible way.

When cognitive dissonance occurs, people attempt to change something to bring harmony to their conflicting experiences. They may alter behavior or reassess their values and attitudes. When people cannot accomplish these alterations or if the alterations still conflict, people remain in distress.

The distress caused by unforgivable injuries involves beliefs about harm and control and about oneself, others, and God as they are related to harm and control. If a Pilot in Command believes he is in control of injury and finds out that his subordinate was quite capable of dealing a severe blow, the Pilot might give up one idea or the other—either that he controls injury or that the subordinate cannot injure him.

If you have believed you are vulnerable to everyone except your protector and the protector injures you, you must give up one belief or the other—that you are immune to injury at the hands of the protector or that protectors never injure.

If you have assumed, as a Mathematician might, that your kind behavior toward others will protect you from being wounded, you will need either to reject the idea that your behavior is linked to protection from harm or conclude that you have not yet found the right way to assure your protection. If kindness did not protect you, maybe something else will.

Buck and Amanda believed that their contributions to the community—their caring child rearing, their hospitality to teenagers, and their belief in God—would assure their happiness. They also believed that God would protect them. After their son died, Amanda confessed this:

> *I'm still angry with God. He gave us only Ted. If he had intended to take Ted, he should have given us a few spares. We never used anything to prevent the birth of more children in all those years. And that's cruel. He is better in my mind now because we have Jason now. God's getting his head screwed on.*

Something about their belief in themselves and their contribution to others, their belief in God, or both had to give. The ideas became compatible.

In the transformation of forgiveness, forgivers construct a new overarching principle about life. The principle, however it is constructed, works to help a person again be able to perceive life as inherently just and fair. The principle resolves incompatibility among beliefs about personal harm. I call this the *forgiveness principle*.

THE FORGIVENESS PRINCIPLE

People who go through the conversion of forgiveness arrive at this conclusion: *Harm is an ever-present potential.*

Like love, fun, or death, harm is part of life. Any harm can be interpreted to make sense, because there is a reason for it and something that controls it. Some harm you can control; some you cannot. Once a person accepts that harm happens and in many respects cannot be controlled, almost nothing can be unforgivable again.

Sarah, whose twelve-year marriage ended abruptly when her husband came home, packed his bags, and left, said this about her new ideas on harm and fairness:

> *My expectations have changed. I'm more reality oriented. I couldn't be amazed by anything. Now infidelity is a part of my phenomenology and framework in the field of possibilities. I think I can anticipate anything.*

Sarah's new forgiveness principle could be stated as follows: "Harm happens. I thought I could control it, but I could not. I will expect it again and know I can transcend it or choose to walk away from it."

Buck and Amanda reformed their idea of God and began to consider reincarnation:

> *This little guy just fell right out of heaven. I think God circled around and threw Ted back to us. The whole story of how we got Jason is almost unreal. If I believed in reincarnation, I'd swear Ted was here. This baby acts just like him.*

Buck and Amanda's forgiveness principle was this: "Harm happens. God has a reason. His reasons are as yet inscrutable to us, but there is some orderly principle working. If there is a reason for all harm, no harm can be unforgivable."

Nicole, who was abused by her domineering and protective husband, concluded this about people and justice after she forgave her husband for abusing her:

> *We're dealing with humans. Humans are self-serving. Most people look out for themselves first. They care about others, but they are lucky just to be able to get through their own lives. Now that I accept that, I accept others' mistakes and my own. I'm freed up as a result.*

Nicole's forgiveness principle is "Harm happens. Anyone can hurt anyone else, including me. I am free because I know this."

Control over the events of one's life, to a person who has forgiven, becomes a matter of accepting that some things are in one's control but others are not. Justice becomes a matter of knowing that harm happens and accepting that you are not immune to it. No one is.

The forgiveness principle does not mean that forgivers are masochists ready to undergo pain at any time. To the contrary, when you have decided that injury is part of life, you can also decide to avoid it when you see it coming or leave it when you think it is unfair or extreme. You will not escape pain or look for it, either; it's just that it will never catch you so off guard again.

THE RELIGIOUS AND EXISTENTIAL FORGIVENESS PARADIGMS

Most of the people I talked to developed forgiveness principles that fall into one of two paradigms about a harmful world. In either paradigm (i.e., a complete and harmonious set of beliefs), personal harm is a constant potential. All the forgivers I talked with acknowledged that they were likely to experience injury again. Moral contracts with new spouses or friends (or redrawn contracts with old acquaintances) could not, no matter how carefully thought out, preclude injuries from happening again. The two paradigms were the same, in other words, where harm was concerned. They differed when control and justice entered in. The first paradigm I call the *existential paradigm*; the second, the *religious paradigm*.

The forgiver who transforms his beliefs into the existential paradigm decides this: Harm comes to everyone; moral contracts between people cannot prevent it; no one is immune to it; and harms come into people's lives almost *randomly*. There is no rhyme or reason to injury. People lie, withhold information, restrict one another's freedom, and are essentially self-oriented. That is the nature of humans. Unintentionally and intentionally, humans harm each other and muddy up each other's lives. The test of your character in the future will be how you react to adversity when it comes your way.

The forgiver who transforms his beliefs into the religious paradigm decides this: Harm comes to everyone; moral contracts cannot prevent injury; no one is immune from it; but a larger force (usually God) has a reason, however mysterious, for injuries that befall people. People may suffer, but the suffering has a larger purpose. The test of a person's character is how well he functions even when he cannot understand God's plan for him.

In either paradigm, the religious or the existential, lies an inherent gift—perhaps the true gift of forgiving. When you forgive, the experiences that happened to you help you understand all interpersonal damage and, paradoxically, feel equipped more than ever to handle it. The hatred you have felt is gone, and the future under its newly constructed beliefs looks brighter because it places intimate injuries into a larger perspective. People who have grappled with forgiveness and accomplished it know they can experience pain and transcend it. Once you know this, you need never be so vigilant about injury again.

The gift of forgiving, then, is the relaxation of vigilance. The new self becomes more relaxed, less defensive and brittle. Forgivers know they can be wounded and have learned to take the idea in as part of their working perceptions of reality. They have experienced the worst of pain. Everything ahead should be much easier.

The Freedom of Forgiveness

I asked forgivers whether they felt anything is unforgivable now. Here are some of their responses:

> *I don't think so. Murder, maybe. I can forgive adultery because I understand why. You know, I've lost everything. It's all been ripped off. I understand it, though; nothing is worth the hating.*

> *No. Everything is forgivable by God. I'm not saying we should open the jails; you can't equate forgiving and condoning. But in God everything is forgivable.*

> *No, nothing is really unforgivable now. I hope I could forgive anything.*

> *Now everything that happens I put to "experience." There's something good that comes out of everything. Like recently, I had some money stolen by someone I thought was my friend. And I thought maybe I should be more careful about selecting friends. You put the situation into perspective, and when anything good comes out of it, you forgive.*

You must forgive everything. Otherwise, this would not be a peaceful place. People, I've come to believe, are basically good; but they run off the rails on occasion.

You really have to just accept people for what they are. Don't try to change them. Forgiveness means developing a whole new philosophy about people. Once I did that, nothing anyone could do could be unforgivable anymore.

I found out that love is an illusion. Relationships between men and women are very false. ALL is an illusion. There is nothing to forgive when you realize that people just create their own falseness.

When I forgave was when I became self-secure and autonomous in my own right. My life was my life, and I thought, I can leave my husband right now, this minute. I am somebody special. To me, the only person I need to forgive is myself and to accept the fact that I have been forgiven by God. God forgives, so you don't have to punish yourself.

I decided I'm not the teacher or the judge of who's a failure or who isn't. I'm not the scorekeeper. Everyone makes mistakes. So I think I MUST forgive.

I don't know that there's anything I couldn't forgive. I've had the worst. And I figure I will also make mistakes, and because I forgave my father, maybe it will make me able to forgive myself some other time.

I know I've hurt people and there will be a judgment for that. But it's not my place to judge. I'll leave that to God. He will take care of it in his own way.

I decided that people are basically good, not evil. They make mistakes, though. You're not obliged to forgive like a Christian might believe, but I choose to forgive. It makes my life peaceful.

Everyone is accountable and will be judged by their deeds. So you're supposed to forgive because everyone has a weakness. You just don't hang around with them.

It is essential to not excuse. You can forgive, but you must not excuse. Excusing means you believe there is some logical reason a person behaves the way he behaves. In cases like incest or beating, there is no logical reason. So excusing is dangerous. If we have free will, we are responsible for ourselves. Granted, things may affect our judgment, but it IS our judgment.

There is no such a thing as imminent justice. People hurt each other all the time. Some are meanspirited, some are manipulative, some are schemers. That's the way it is. So you don't let them have the power to destroy you. You blow them off and go on with your life. Only next time around, you're just much more careful about the choices you make.

PART **III**

Tools for Forgiving

THE ENTIRE PROCESS OF FORGIVING is a process of conversion from being an object of another person's actions to being a person who acts upon her own injury. Through the six phases of the forgiving process, you will gain an ever-increasing mastery over your injury. You build a new belief system about injustice, other people, and yourself.

Just as the pathways to forgiveness are similar, there is another, shared experience among many forgivers, this one sad. Aids that might help promote forgiving are few and far between. Some people seek help in fiction or poetry. Others turn to the Bible, books, or even television talk shows. As if wandering through the rows of a backyard garden, injured people wander through their personal resources looking for anything they can pick out that might help them to heal.

Helpers, both professionals and friends, are able to assist at least some of the time, but many do not see forgiveness as the final goal for a wounded person. Some helpers may not know how to assist people beyond allowing them to vent their feelings or repeat their stories. Only a few people I talked with reported that counselors saw them through the entire process, from beginning to end. More reported that helpers were not helpful at all.

The successful forgivers whose stories are reflected in previous chapters muddled through the process by marshaling whatever resources they could. Almost all said they had tried to find a faster method to help them but did not know how. Not knowing how to forgive, injured people developed various "forgiving exercises" and "forgiving tools" on their own. It is a reflection of human beings' creativity and desire to heal that the tools actually promoted a process of reconciliation. These tools and others will be presented in the next several chapters.

Forgiving tools, like other tools, are useful only if they fit the hand of the user. Some exercises described in the following pages may be useful for some people but not to others. They are meant to foster individual creativity. Both injured people and professional counselors who help them may find the exercises useful as they are presented here or may choose to modify them to fit a given situation.

The exercises have been designed to take the injured person progressively through the forgiving process, from naming through the emergence of a new self. They reflect the techniques and methods chosen by those who completed the process by themselves and those who got assistance from friends, counselors, reflection, or prayer. Additional exercises that might facilitate rapid progression through the various phases of forgiving are also offered.

CHAPTER **10**

Tools for Naming the Injury

> Order and simplification are the first steps toward mastery of a subject—the actual enemy is the unknown.
>
> THOMAS MANN

N aming the injury is the first step on the journey to forgiveness. Out of the confusion of the injury's aftermath, naming begins to order and identify what has been lost and what remains intact. The objective of the naming phase is to make completely clear the previously hidden dimensions of the wound. What beliefs have been permanently altered? How have a person's concepts of vulnerability, control, and justice changed because of the injury? What, precisely, needs to be forgiven?

Naming clarifies the previously obscured. It orders the nature of the forgiving process that lies ahead. Once you have fully named your injury, you can start down the road to mastering your wound rather than allowing it to overwhelm you.

Admitting, exploring, and talking are the three tasks of naming

175

an injury. The exercises that follow are designed to help you complete these tasks so you can know what you must contend with as you try to forgive.

Preparation for Forgiving

Before you begin the process of forgiving, some preparation is in order. First, be prepared to work; prepare to take time to think about your situation and to take action. Second, throughout the process, you will need to keep notes and complete exercises. A notebook or journal is a good vehicle for recording your responses to exercises and charting your progress. Keeping a "forgiving notebook" allows you to spend special time working at forgiving. Special time set aside for forgiveness work might make thoughts about the injury less likely to creep into your everyday activities and mar your daily functioning.

The first exercise is designed to develop the habit of thinking about the unforgivable injury in an orderly way. When you order your thoughts about the injury, you can watch the ways your presumptions about it change over time.

Exercise 1: Framing the Injury

In your forgiving notebook write down the event that precipitated your unforgivable injury. Write everything you remember about it. Where were you when it happened? What were you wearing? How were you feeling? What were your first thoughts after it happened? How old were you? Whose faces do you remember? What color do you see? What physical sensations do you feel now as you think about it?

You might also choose to tape-record this exercise so that you can return to it later and see how you are changing in your understanding of the unforgivable event and the injuries that followed.

The next exercise, also preparatory, will help you gauge how your current perceptions of yourself and your injurer have already changed. Like exercise 1, this is one you will return to during the forgiving process to chart the progress you are making. Try it now to give yourself a baseline assessment of your changing expectations.

Exercise 2: "I thought I was _____."

Write down the following statements and complete the sentences. You might want to share these sentences with a friend or therapist.

Before he did that to me, I thought I was _____.
I thought I would _____.
I thought he was _____.
I thought he would _____.
I thought we were _____.
I thought we would _____.
Since he did that to me, I think I am _____.
I think I will _____.
I think he is _____.
I think he will _____.
I think we were _____.
I think we will _____.

Once you have completed the first two exercises, you have set the stage for the remainder of the naming exercises. They are designed to help you admit, explore, and talk about your current perceptions of yourself and your situation. The exercises address your changing views about vulnerability, control, and justice. They also help you begin to identify strengths you may be developing. When you complete them, you may have begun to come to grips with the "changing you." You will also be introduced to the ideas you must reassess and redefine as you go through the remainder of the forgiving process.

Admitting Exercises

ADMITTING VULNERABILITY

An unforgivable injury significantly affects an injured person's ideas about his own vulnerability to harm. As difficult as it may be, such a wound leaves most people feeling completely vulnerable and out of control, some for the first time in their lives. Still, vulnerability is a two-edged sword. You might find out you were vulnerable when you thought you were not; and you might find that vulnerability will open up new possibilities for you. Complete exercises 3, 4, and 5 to assess current thoughts about vulnerability in general (not just vulnerability to your offender).

Exercise 3: "I never thought I could be hurt by _____."

Complete the following thoughts:

1. I never thought I could be hurt by (name at least five things or people) _____.
2. I never thought that being hurt could make me _____.
3. I thought I was safe in (or with) _____.

Exercise 4: Draw a Picture

Draw a picture of how you think of yourself right now. Try to detail where you are, what form you take, how large you are, and who or what else is present.

What do you see in the picture about your feelings of vulnerability?

Exercise 5: "This is just like _____."

Sometimes new injuries bring back feelings of vulnerability people have experienced at other times in their lives. Complete this sentence to see if you have felt the way you do now at some earlier time in your life. "The way I feel today reminds me of how I felt when ———————."

Exercise 6: Pilot in Command, Defenseless Drifter, or Mathematician?

Pilots in Command are shocked by their vulnerability to subordinates. Defenseless Drifters are vulnerable when they are abandoned by the strong people around them. Mathematicians are vulnerable when their equations about life do not work. Which type are you?

Write a short admission letter in your notebook about the person who hurt you. How did you view the injurer in relation to you? What role did you play? Start the letter with this, addressed to your injurer:

Dear————,
 I know I was vulnerable to you, but I never knew you could
 ——————————.

Do not mail this "letter." Instead, keep it in your notebook.

The sudden jolt that comes when you are shocked by your own vulnerability can be staggering. The more trusting you have become over time and the longer your moral history is with friends, parents, children, or spouses, the more likely time has lulled you into a sense of false invulnerability. Try to remember, though, that it was vulnerability to intimate people that made your relationship special in the first place. Admitting vulnerability to harm does not make you weak. Instead, it probably means that you were caught off guard. If you can admit nothing else, try to admit to yourself that the injury was unforgivable partly because you were caught off guard by your own capacity to be harmed. If you can do so, write about this in your notebook. Vulnerability may not be at the heart of unforgivable injuries; not recognizing your own vulnerabilities, on the other hand, may be.

ADMITTING CONFUSION ABOUT CONTROL

Most people want to feel in control of the most important aspects of their personal lives. People want to control whom they live, work, and play with and whom they love. Unforgivable injuries strip people of control over one or many of these personal choices. While it is initially frightening to feel out of control, it is important to recognize that there are many things you can still regulate. It is also vital to recognize that later on you will think differently—perhaps even more realistically—about control. For the moment, take time to do the next exercise to remind yourself that you maintain control over some very important aspects of your life.

Exercise 7: "I Am in Control" Checklist

Check which of these decisions or events you still have control over. In your notebook, add your own items.
I can control

———— 1. When I get up in the morning.

———— 2. When I leave for work (or to see friends, go shopping, etc.).

———— 3. My emotions, if only for five minutes (ten minutes, etc.).

———— 4. Whether someone loves me or not.

———— 5. Whether someone likes me.

———— 6. Whether I lie to someone.

———— 7. What I will wear today.

———— 8. Whether I will call a friend today.

———— 9. Whether I call a professional to get help today.

———— 10. What I watch on television or listen to on my cassette player (or radio or CD).

———— 11. How I treat my children (friends, parents, co-workers).

——— 12. Whether I exercise today (take a warm bath, eat a favorite food).

Exercise 8: "I used to control _____, or so I thought."

The events and decisions you thought you had control over or could prevent are in a state of flux. Complete the following thoughts.

1. I used to think I could control _____.
2. I used to think I could prevent _____.

Exercise 9: "I can't control you."

Imagine the person who injured you. Think of this person's face (or look at a picture if you have one).

When you are ready, say out loud to the picture or imaginary person:

I cannot control you. I can't control what you think or what you do. I cannot control whether you love me or hurt me in the past. Today, though, I can control myself.

Use your own words and elaborate on what you *can* control.

ADMITTING THAT JUSTICE IS NOT WHAT YOU THOUGHT

Everyone has an idea about how justice works. Many people believe that harm does not come to those who do not somehow deserve to be harmed. Take time to assess what is happening to your thoughts about justice.

Exercise 10: Essay on Justice

Write down in your notebook at least three rules you believe about justice.

Then write a short "essay" about these rules. How did you come to believe in them? Do they still work for you? What do you think you will have to change about your ideas on justice?

If you can, share these thoughts with a friend or support group.

Finally, after many unforgivable injuries, people hold the deep fear that part of themselves will never be the same. Something has been taken away that can never be restored.

Exercise 11: The Lost (and Found?)

If you feel that part of you will never be the same, try to identify what it is. Search for it. Is it faith, compassion, hope? Later on, you will need to work very hard to recover what has been taken from you. If you can identify it now, do so.

Exploring Exercises

When you explore your injury further, you will begin to find its boundaries and limits. Not only have your current ideas about vulnerability, control, and justice been affected, but also your ideas about the future are changing. Exploring the injury introduces you to how the future looks different now. As you explore further, you will also begin to see strengths emerging from the injury. The exercises below are designed to help you to see your changing ideas on the future and to identify which feelings still remain intact.

Exercise 12: The Futures Letter

Imagine yourself as you were before you were hurt. Write a "futures letter." In the letter describe to a friend your future as you imagined it before the injury. Talk about your hopes and dreams for yourself (and your family, if it applies). Reveal your private wishes and desires. If you were a child when you were unforgivably wounded, write from the viewpoint of the child before the hurt (even if that seems hard to do). In this letter, talk about what you thought life would be like.

After you have written the letter, read it once. Then put it away. If you can, share it with a friend or counselor. Once you know how you saw your future before the injury, you can determine which part you can still try to accomplish and which parts you must put aside.

Exercise 13: "I may be hurt, but I still feel _____."

Even when you believe your future has been devastated, you are still intact. So are many of your feelings. As you go through the days after your injury, write down in your notebook an ongoing list of feelings you still enjoy. The title of your notebook page should be the same as the exercise title.

An example might be:

I may be hurt, but I still feel
1. Happy to see a rainbow.
2. Relieved when my best friend comes over.
3. Lucky to have a family, etc.

Try to identify any positive feelings you may be experiencing.

TALKING AS AN EXERCISE

You have probably talked to someone by now about your unforgivable wound. Talking, as I said in chapter 4, helps you place the events of your life in a logical sequence. It validates your perceptions of the injury. It assists you to see that another person cares. Talking also helps you steer clear of taking actions that might bring about more damage.

The person you choose to talk to should be patient, wise, non-judgmental, and not afraid of your emotions—whether they are emotions of grief and pain or hate and rage. A good listener is also respectful of your perceptions of the injury. Avoid someone who challenges or invalidates your experiences.

When you talk, you hear your own story. If you talk about the issues you have addressed in these exercises, you will be able to describe the injury and the impact it had on your relationship with the one who hurt you. You can tell another person about your changing ideas on vulnerability, control, and justice, including your ideas about what you still *can* control.

If you are able to tell someone about your future and how it now seems totally changed, do that also.

DIVERSIONS LISTS

Give yourself a daily breather from focusing on your process of forgiving. Diversions are especially important during this part of the healing process. At the beginning of each week, once you start the forgiving process, list in your notebook at least five activities that force you to think about something other than yourself for at least an hour. If your mind wanders during quiet activities (e.g., reading), do not include these activities in your diversions list. Activities likely to take your mind away from your problems usually include other people or physical participation.

Exercise 14: Diversions

Select from your diversions list one activity. Decide on a specific time and date for engaging in this project. Then follow through. Below is a list of some diversions that might work for you.

1. Play bridge (chess, checkers, rummy, or any other game) with a group of friends.
2. Invite friends over for a simple meal and a movie on the VCR.
3. Volunteer to coach Special Olympics athletes (Girl Scouts, Boy Scouts, a church group, or other children's group).
4. Take a group piano (guitar, voice, banjo, kazoo) lesson at a local community college or YMCA.
5. Join a group engaged in cleaning up the environment in your local area. Go on a cleanup weekend.
6. Go bird-watching (wind sailing, roller-skating, horseback riding) with a club or a group of friends.
7. If you are like many people, you have pictures lying around that need to be put into albums. Invite friends over to a night of organizing photographs. Each person can bring a box of photographs and albums. You furnish munchies.
8. Go to a lecture (book-reading session, county-extension-agent presentation) and learn something new.
9. Listen to someone else's troubles.
10. Play racquetball (tennis, horseshoe, shuffleboard, volleyball).

You can find diversions of your own; but try to engage in something outside your work that gives you some relief from the stress you are experiencing. Even those who work hardest at healing need to rest. Find a constructive way to do it. (Since sleep is likely to be a problem, anyhow, during this time, you should know that alcohol only exacerbates sleep disturbances.) Find diversions that are healthy and not disruptive to your daily routine. You will need to moderate both eating and drinking so that your body *can* rest when your mind allows it to.

Naming the injury requires a delicate balance between confronting changes you are experiencing and hanging on to your strengths and hopes. It requires a relaxing of denial and an acknowledgment that change is on the horizon. It is vital that you go at your own pace, though. It is not useful to hurry when you are not ready. This is true in any of the forgiving phases. Use these tools when you are ready. Like a scar healing on skin, every psychological wound heals at its own pace. You can gauge the pace through working on your process of forgiving, one phase at a time.

Naming an injury organizes, simplifies, and orders your thoughts about being harmed. Once the full wound is known, the enemy of confusion gives way to the direction you must begin to take in order to forgive. You know what you do not believe anymore; now you must move forward to developing beliefs that once again make sense to you and bring you peace. Naming the injury is like looking into a clear lake when the winds quiet in the evening dusk and the waves settle into a mirror. Now you can see each detail on the bottom clearly. You know where you have to dive to pick up a beautiful stone on the bottom. Once you can see things clearly, the next efforts are simpler.

11

Tools for Claiming the Injury

This is your life now. What do you want to do with it?
JOAN

In the naming phase of forgiving, you began to recognize that your life was changing, even if the changes were against your will. You stop fighting these changes in the claiming phase and begin, instead, to make them work in your behalf. In a sense, when you claim something, it becomes a part of you. When you claim an unforgivable injury, you take it inside. Once claimed, it is a part of who you are from then on.

We said in chapter 7 that the two tasks of claiming are separating and incorporation. Separating an injury helps you tease out which part of the injury is yours alone. Incorporation helps you stop fighting off the permanency of the changes caused by the injury, to accept them and make them an ongoing part of your identity.

Standing in the way of these tasks are demands on resources, confused ego boundaries, and plain fear—especially fear of internalizing something bitter and painful. Offsetting these barriers is the recognition that even in the early stages of forgiveness, good things can happen if you only look for them. You are learning skills, revisiting your values, and encountering new resources.

The first exercise of the claiming phase is designed to help you recognize any good that may trickle out of the pain you are enduring.

Exercise 1: The Gift List

As you heal, you will become more aware that every tragedy bears its own gifts. Right now, though, gifts may be too difficult to recognize. You will heal faster and forgive more quickly if you can begin to see good things that result from bad circumstances.

Set aside a portion of your "forgiving notebook" in which to record these positive results. Entitle it "The Gift List." Starting today, try to think of any unexpected benefit that has come your way because of what has happened to you. (You may label categories, like "new friends," "new skills," "renewed values," "renewed friendships," "experiences that would not have happened had the injury not occurred," and so forth.) At the end of each day for a few weeks, turn to your gift list. Try to think whether the day offered up anything hopeful or encouraging. On days you feel particularly down, look over the list. Make yourself consider the good along with the bad, as difficult as that may seem. Add to the list as often as you can.

Forgiving is the process of giving yourself and the person who injured you a gift of freedom. The more quickly you recognize how many friends, skills, and values you have acquired from the wound, the faster you will find that freedom. The gift-list exercise gives you a format in which you can begin to survey your personal resources. Then you can start to separate your injury from the injuries that affected other people as a result of the unforgivable event.

Separating

In order to understand exactly what you must cope with and incorporate and how you must change, you need to assess which moral rules were disrupted by the injurer. What moral notions will you find it difficult to place faith in, in the future? Have you given up on truthfulness? Loyalty? Mercy? What has the injury done to you (at least for now) and your sense of morality? The next exercise is designed to help you assess your particular losses.

Exercise 2: Lost-and-Found Ad

If you were to place an ad in the Lost and Found section of your local newspaper, what would you write about your losses? For example:

Lost: Belief in people. Belief in justice. On Friday, March 7. If you have found them, please call.

Now imagine the others who were hurt in the injury. What has each of them lost? How are their losses separate and different from yours? You can forgive only your own injury, not someone else's. Similarly, others hurt by the same circumstances must do their own forgiveness work. You cannot do it for them.

To identify what parts of the unforgivable injury were unique to you alone, you need to consider your moral relationship and special moral agreements with the offender. What did the two of you hold sacred? How did that come to be? Did you agree that certain behaviors were taboo and would not be tolerated? Try this exercise to clarify how your *particular* moral agreements with the offender were violated by the unforgivable injury.

Exercise 3: A Moral History

Write the story of your history with the offender. Instead of recounting things you did and events in your life, write about how you two decided together what was right and wrong behavior for the two of you.

Were there any agreements about your rules of right and wrong? Did either of you break one of the rules before? What did you do about that breach? As part of your story, make sure to include three separate sections: (1) beliefs you are positive you at one time shared and agreed not to violate, (2) beliefs about right and wrong you know you had disagreements about, and (3) gray areas, where you are not sure what the offender believed.

When you were unforgivably hurt, is it clear that the action was wrong? What effect do you currently think the injury will have on your ideas about right and wrong in general?

The other people who were hurt by the injury may have become mixed into your perceptions of the harm. It is difficult in a ruptured marriage, for example, to separate your hurt from the hurt your children might also experience. Parents often feel, exquisitely at times, their children's pain. Still, children of a ruptured marriage will have different wounds to forgive.

If you were injured during your childhood, you may never have completely disentangled your wounds from those of your parents or brothers and sisters. Try these next exercises to help you separate your injury from those experienced by other people.

Exercise 4: Fallout List

Option 1. Make a "fallout list." On this list, identify everyone who was hurt in the injury. In one or two sentences, tell how each was hurt. Include yourself in the list. How were your injuries different from everyone else's? Tell someone about these differences.

Option 2. On separate index cards, write the name of every person who was hurt by the unforgivable injury. Arrange these cards into a circle and one by one place the names into its center. Imagine what each person on the outside circle might say to give comfort to the person in the middle. When you put your own card in the center, allow others to comfort you. What might each person say to you?

Exercise 5: Photo Therapy

This exercise is especially useful if the injurer is dead or if the injury happened long ago.

Take out old photographs of yourself and other members of your family (or whoever your injurer was). Try to get as many different groupings of people in the photographs as you can (brothers and sisters together, mothers and fathers, grandparents). Try to find one of yourself at the age at which you were injured. Who was with you in these pictures? How did you look? How did others look? Who was sitting next to whom? Why? What were the expressions on everyone's faces? What do you think each person was thinking and feeling? How did you feel at the time these pictures were taken? How did all of these people make you feel when the injuries were going on? Point out the injurers. Do this task with a friend or therapist.

Why were you uniquely affected by the unforgivable events? What *exactly* do you have to forgive? How is your wound different from other people's in the photograph?

Exercise 6: Give Yourself a Break

Many people feel overwhelmed by demands on their time and resources just when they need more of both to work on forgiving. In this exercise, write down all of the demands that take away from your healing process:

DEMANDS	POTENTIAL SOLUTIONS
1. _____	_____
2. _____	_____
3. _____	_____
4. _____	_____
5. _____	_____
6. _____	_____

In a corresponding list, write down any methods you could use to unburden yourself of the demands. Could you, for example, ask friends for help? Could you divvy up some of your chores at home among your children? Could you form car pools to save money? Are neighborhood telephone hot lines feasible to help working parents keep better track of their children?

If you need to, ask friends or family members for ideas. Take the "demands lists" to a support group you attend. Find ways to give yourself time to develop more resources so that balancing the scale (further along in the forgiving process) will be easier.

Incorporation

The next group of exercises is designed to help you begin to accept the part of you that is to change permanently because of the injury. The intent of incorporation is to accept what you cannot change (while retaining your strengths).

In this exercise, you will look back at your life to recognize how both the painful and difficult parts and the gentle, loving, and pleasurable parts have created the person you are at this moment. You have had difficult times before the unforgivable injury; and they have become part of you. The unforgivable injury must become part of you as well.

Exercise 7: Placing Your Injurer in Perspective

1. The person who hurt you is one small piece of your life, not the sum total of it. Write down the names of every person you consider a major contributor to the person you have become. Include important friends, teachers, family members, significant adults, children, neighbors, church members, and so forth. Think about how important all of these people have been to you. (If you have lost track of some of them, perhaps you might want to reestablish contact.) It is likely that these people have contributed to your life in as significant a way as—or perhaps more significantly than—the injurer has. Try to put the injurer in perspective when you think about these other very important people.

2. Write down a list of people whose lives you have been a very important part of. Sometimes it is too easy, particularly when a person is in pain, to forget how meaningful your life has been to other people. You are an important part of many other people's lives. Your contributions have been unique. Take time to recognize how special you have been to others. You have participated in making other people's lives what they are, just as other people have participated in making yours what it is. Take the opportunity to review your contributions.

3. Spend an evening with a new friend. As you talk about your life, describe the people who have been important to you. Reminiscence can be a healing experience. Describe special memories and moments in your life. Include the injurer, but discuss others as well. You are a

part of *all* of your experiences. The claiming phase of forgiving is the time to begin to remind yourself of this.

There are still wishes in your heart and dreams for your future that you had hoped to experience with the injurer. These have been altered and most likely will never be fulfilled. You must absorb or incorporate your unfulfilled dreams and hopes. But, at the same time, you must develop new dreams for yourself. It is not the loss of hope that you must incorporate, but instead the loss of a *specific* hope.

The next exercise is designed to help you incorporate a new resolve to set your sights again on goals and hopes, but this time without the injurer (or with the injurer but toward a different dream). You will work hard to accomplish this, but there will be other people along the way to help you realize new hopes and dreams later on.

Exercise 8: The Wishes Exercise

Write down the wishes your wound leaves unfulfilled. (E.g., "I wish I could look forward to taking that trip we talked about." Or, "I wish my children had become what I'd hoped for." Or, "I wish my childhood had been as happy as I used to think it was.") Can you do anything to make these wishes come true? If not, rewrite them. Only this time, state them as they might be changed in the future. For example:

"I can no longer hope to take a trip with _____ *again, but I can afford* _____*." "I can no longer believe my childhood was perfect, but I can believe* _____*."*

It may seem hard to wish right now, but your wish lists will get longer again as you continue toward forgiving.

The next three exercises are designed to help you think about the changes you have undergone that you should accept as permanent parts of your life. Try one or more of these exercises; remember your strengths underlie the changes you will be making; and change, if it is toward forgiveness, is positive.

Exercise 9: Obituary Writing

On a piece of paper, write an obituary for your old relationship with your injurer. Include good and bad times. Then describe the part of you that has ended because of the injury. (Example: "Since December 6, I am no longer naive. On that day, my childish naïveté died.") Show the obituary to a friend or a counselor. If it's comfortable for you, send it to someone you know or to yourself in the mail.

Exercise 10: Lifeline Exercise

On a piece of paper, draw a horizontal line and label it "lifeline" (fig. 4). Next, use a zigzag line to record the ups and downs of your life. Peaks above the line indicate high

Fig. 4 Example of a Lifeline

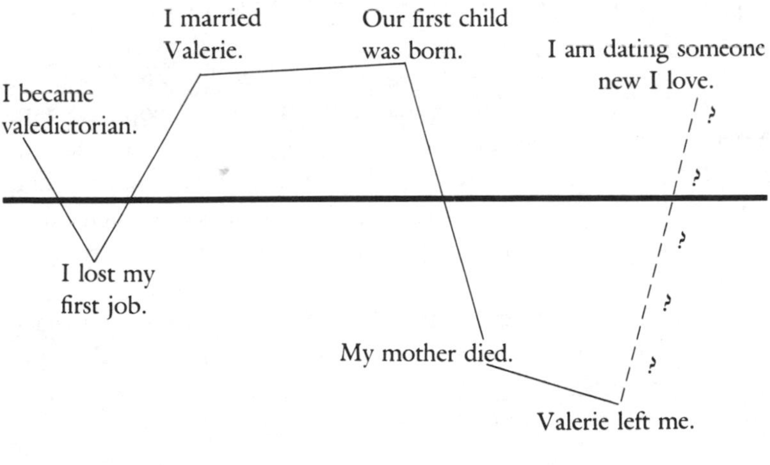

points; valleys below the line indicate low points. Look at your life since the unforgivable injury. Try to imagine what the next peak might be (e.g., a new job or a new love affair) and plot it with a dotted line. Try to imagine yet another peak.

Exercise 11: The Life Raft Exercise

Imagine that a flood is coming and you can gather up everyone who makes you safe and put them into a life raft along with provisions enough to last for a year. Where is your injurer—in or out of the raft?

1. If out of the raft, push the life raft off from the shore. What happens to everyone else?
2. If in the raft, push off from shore. What happens to everyone else?
3. If in the raft, make your injurer go to the shore and push off. What happens to everyone else in the life raft?

From this exercise, you should be able to see whether your dreams of safety and trust have been altogether altered because you have been wounded. What are they now?

Separating and incorporating your injury can be hard work. No one wants to claim something that hurts. But what people do with bitter aspects of their lives (and with the rage and grief that accompany bitter experiences) presents a true test of their character and determination. To be a person of grace and integrity when life is going well is one thing; to be a person of grace and integrity when life has dealt a particularly bitter blow is quite another. When you claim your injury, you acknowledge that life's tragedies and joys have combined to make you who you are. You will become what you decide to become.

12

Tools for Blaming the Injurer

When my best friend had an affair with my husband, I knew I
was responsible, but *she* was to blame. . . .

MARY

Blaming means that you assign responsibility to someone for
causing an incident to happen and acknowledge that the behavior was wrong. Blaming is not raging or whining. It is not childish
or self-centered. Blaming brings confusion into focus and clarifies
who an injurer really is. It lets you know whom to forgive.

As discussed in chapter 6, there are three tasks of blaming: filtering,
weighing, and fact-finding. The end product of these tasks is a conclusion about who is to blame for the unforgivable injury and who
is not. Almost always the completion of these tasks of blaming brings
you to one conclusion: The injurer is to blame. You may have contributed to events (as does everyone who participates at all); but
usually one person alone violated a moral agreement. One person
alone could have anticipated that such behavior might bring about

an unforgivable wound. When you conclude that the injurer probably meant to injure, your myths about this person must now give
way to fact. You must relinquish the excuses you have made for him
and face the truth: The person who hurt you is not who you had
hoped he would be. He is the one who changed your life permanently. You must begin to let go.

Exercises in the blaming phase of forgiving help you in another
of the eight conversions—from a person who is the object of someone's will to a person who acts upon someone else. Self-blame gives
way to other-blame. Other-blame puts you in the position of acting
rather than thinking about what you might have done to prevent
the unforgivable injury. To begin this conversion, though, you might
want to assess your current ideas about blaming.

Exercise 1: *Your Blaming History*

Each of us has a certain style of placing responsibility on
ourselves or something outside ourselves when events happen.[1] Some people routinely hold themselves responsible
when they fall short of their own expectations. Other people
in the same circumstances hold external forces responsible
for the same outcome. Try to figure out which style of
placing responsibility you tend to follow.

Return to the Lifeline Exercise in chapter 11. From your
lifeline, identify your five most important accomplishments.
Next, identify your five most disappointing experiences. List
the ten experiences in a column. In a corresponding column,
check who (or what) you believe was most responsible for
your accomplishments or disappointments *at the time they
happened.* Who or what do you consider most responsible
now for each of these experiences?

Can you find any pattern in the ways you assigned responsibility in the past? Is there a pattern now? Are these patterns
reflected in the way you are assigning blame in your unforgivable injury?

Who Is Responsible for Your
Accomplishments or Disappointments?

WHO DID YOU BELIEVE WAS RESPONSIBLE AT THE TIME?			
ACCOMPLISHMENTS	YOURSELF	ANOTHER (OTHERS)	THE SITUATION (luck, higher power, chance)
1.			
2.			
3.			
4.			
5.			
DISAPPOINTMENTS			
1.			
2.			
3.			
4.			
5.			
WHO DO YOU NOW BELIEVE IS RESPONSIBLE?			
ACCOMPLISHMENTS	YOURSELF	ANOTHER (OTHERS)	THE SITUATION (luck, higher power, chance)
1.			
2.			
3.			
4.			
5.			
DISAPPOINTMENTS			
1.			
2.			
3.			
4.			
5.			

You will need to decide in your own mind once and for all who caused this injury to happen so that you can ultimately forgive those who did. To accomplish the filtering task, try this exercise:

Exercise 2: Filtering

> In your notebook, write a list of everyone you could conceivably imagine was responsible for your wound. First, think of "distant" people who might have influenced the unforgivable event. Next, identify all of the possible "recent" contributors. Then do this:
>
> 1. Cross off the list the name of anyone you believe simply cannot be held responsible for your wound.
> 2. Order the names that remain from most to least responsible.
>
> Once you have completed this ordering, you will want to consider whether your own style of blaming has any bearing on whom you hold responsible for this injury.

Now that you have isolated those people you believe to be most responsible, ask yourself the next question: Did any of these individuals engage in behavior that was wrong? Did any violate a moral agreement? To do this, try the next exercise.

Exercise 3: "My injurer did something that was _____."

> 1. Select the final word of the following sentence from the list below. "When my injurer hurt me, he did something that was _____." (You may add other adjectives if you choose.)

> silly   careless
> thoughtless   cruel

selfish	sadistic
malicious	foolish
inept	dangerous
rash	mean

Each is an adjective describing the action that precipitated the unforgivable event. For example:

When Mary hurt me, she did something that was thoughtless.

For each person you decided may be responsible for the unforgivable injury, complete the sentence.

2. Look over your sentences. Did any person do something that stands out as being more wrong than the others? Is it clear that some people might have been foolish (or even selfish) but not in violation of any definition of wrong that you shared?

Once you have identified those who were more wrong than others in their actions, it is time to move to the second task of blaming: *weighing*. In this task, you decide who could have foreseen that his actions might result in an unforgivable wound and who, if anyone, engaged in actions that intentionally brought about the injury.

Exercise 4: The Rungs of Blame

Draw lines in your notebook, one above the other, that correspond to the calibration marks on a Responsibility Scale (see chapter 6). The lower levels represent less responsibility than the higher ones (see fig. 5).

In the last exercise, you identified everyone who contributed to the injury. Now, next to the contribution rung on your Responsibility Scale, write all of the names. From the list, decide which ones could have known that their actions might result in the unforgivable injury. Write the names

Fig. 5 Responsibility Scale

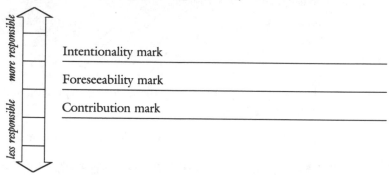

next to the foreseeability rung. You may slide names up and down the rungs several times as you decide appropriate levels of responsibility for each contributor. Next, decide if any of the names in the foreseeability rung intended the unforgivable injury to happen. If you believe that anyone intentionally created the situation, move that person's name to the intentionality rung on your scale. If you cannot be sure of a person's intentions, put a question mark by that name.

Now look at the Responsibility Scale. The name highest on the scale is the one you believe to be most responsible for your injury. Was that person also wrong? Did he violate a moral agreement? If someone was more responsible than others and more wrong, it is this person you will attempt to forgive. If you decide that several people could have foreseen the injury but only one took wrong action, that person is the one whom you will attempt to forgive if you choose to do so.*

Sometimes it is not immediately clear who among the contributors to an event could have foreseen its happening. If you need more help deciding who might have "seen things coming," try this exercise:

---

* If more than one person could have foreseen the injury but none was wrong, then the situation may not call for forgiveness. It may have "just happened." For example, if spouses grow away from each other but no one lied, misled, or used

Exercise 5: The "You Should Have Known" Letter

Write a letter to the injurer. Accuse him of knowing that his behavior might result in the injury. If you want to do so, write a letter back to yourself denying the accusation.

Does your accusation ring true? Is there any way the injurer could *not* have foreseen the results of his actions? If he could have foreseen the results, were his actions wrong? What are your feelings about writing the letter? If you wrote a denial letter, does the denial seem valid?

Exercise 6: The "I Didn't Mean to" Exercise

Have a friend or counselor play the role of your injurer. Have him try to convince you that he could not have anticipated that what he did could cause you such pain. Have him tell you, "I didn't mean to." How did you feel? Did the excuse seem legitimate or not legitimate? Why?

If you are still having trouble deciding if anyone did something intentional to cause the unforgivable injury, try the next exercise.

Exercise 7: Photo Blame

Sort through your old photographs again. Find a picture of the person who hurt you. In a place where you feel comfortable talking to a picture (you may want to be alone for this!), tell the picture you think he hurt you intentionally. Tell it how angry you are. Explain exactly what the person did to you. Say, "It's your fault. I did not deserve this." Repeat that if you want to. How did you feel afterward?

---

the other person, forgiveness is not the right notion. We cannot forgive each other for who we are but only for a wrong action we take that wounds the other. If you decide that no one is responsible, there is no one to forgive. You must resolve to go on with your life without focusing on the incident that probably hurt you both.

It is common for people who are being blamed to offer justifications for their behavior. A common justification is "If you had not done what you did, I would not have done what I did." If an injured person believes the justification arguments of an offender, it will be even more difficult to place blame. During the fact-finding task of blaming, justifications are examined. When they are, evidence usually reveals that an injurer's justifications are faulty. In fact, actions that cause unforgivable injuries are probably integral parts of an injurer's repertoire of behavior. There may be a variety of circumstances that precipitate these actions in people; but, at least among adults, it is unlikely that one person triggers totally new behavior in another person. When justifications are put forward by an injurer, fact-finding exercises might assist an injured person to consider those justifications more objectively.

Exercise 8: Justification Stacks

On cards or pieces of paper, list separately every excuse or justification your injurer has given for the reason he harmed you. Now place the cards in three separate stacks. In the first stack, place the justifications that you do not accept. In the second stack, place justifications you are tempted to accept. In the third stack, place the justifications you accept as valid.

1. Do the stacks make sense?
2. Try to give an argument for and against the justification in the third stack.
3. If these justifications were removed, would your injurer *definitely not* have harmed you in the way that he did? Ask a friend to argue for and against the justifications in stack 3. (Example: You might put this justification in stack 3: "My mother hit me because she was angry that I wore the wrong shoes to school. She had told me not

to wear the shoes, so I deserved to get hit." Would your mother probably have hit you anyhow, even if you had not worn the shoes? Did she use the shoes as an excuse to batter you? Might she have used another justification if you had worn other shoes that day?)

Exercise 9: Library Work

Go to your public library and find books about your specific injury. This is particularly important if your injurer's behavior had anything to do with alcohol or drug dependency, transvestism, bisexuality, homosexuality, battering, or mood disorders like manic depression. In addition to books, you might want to seek out the help of knowledgeable professionals with whom to discuss these situations or disorders. Some disorders may justify certain behavior (or at least make it more understandable). This does not mean that people who have been harmed by others who have alcohol or drug dependencies or mental disorders are any less in pain. It sometimes can mean that blame at the level of intentionality, at least, may not be appropriate. For example, if your cocaine-dependent child steals the only jewelry you inherited from your grandparents and sells it, you may feel great loss and betrayal. Reading about cocaine addiction, though, may help lessen the pain because you understand that drug dependency drove the theft and not your child's enmity toward you.

Once you have filtered, weighed, and done some fact-finding, you can probably draw this conclusion: The injurer is to blame, and you are not. In any intimate relationship, people make mistakes. They may occasionally say or do unkind, selfish, or thoughtless things. One person, at some time in any friendship or family, will not please another. Failing to please, thoughtlessness, or even selfishness, however, are ordinarily not unforgivable. These things are not outside the boundaries of most people's moral expectations of others. They may cause unpleasantness or unhappy exchanges, but they do not violate codes of moral conduct. One person usually does that. It is that person who is wrong and that person who can be blamed.

The tasks of blaming, accomplished through these exercises (and others you may devise yourself), serve to show an injured person that self-blame is self-defeating. Self-blame may give a false sense of control over matters during the days and months just after the injury happens. Self-blame holds out the hope that there are things you can rectify or correct to restore the relationship ruptured by the unforgivable injury. Once self-blame becomes other-blame, though, it follows that only the one who is to blame for an injury can take steps to repair its damage. Only he can apologize or make promises or attempt to make things right again. To blame someone is to accept that the next move toward reaffirming the relationship is in the hands of the one who is blamed; and that is unlikely to happen. In that way, blaming is giving up control—at least control over the relationship between yourself and the one who harmed you. Unless the harmer makes a move to reconcile the relationship, no move *can* be made. When you blame another, you give up control over one thing (your relationship) and begin to take charge of something else. You begin to reestablish control over your own life. Blaming, once done, allows you to begin to work on your life again. In this sense, blaming is a paradoxical part of healing.

CHAPTER **13**

Tools for Balancing the Scales

Intellectually, then, I knew I had to forgive him. The way I did it was to get my own life happy, with a lot of time and a lot of work. When I was happy with me, I could forgive him.

JANET

Any unforgivable injury puts the injured into a position of disadvantage. In the fourth phase of forgiving, balancing the scales, the harmed individual begins to restore advantages to herself. She "balances the scales" with her harmer once again.

Each of the three ordinary methods of balancing the scales—punishment, mock punishment, and loading—involves different activities. The main barrier to their completion is that they require more activity than tasks in the other phases. An output of energy is required. By now, though, if you have successfully completed the other phases, you should have more than enough energy to accomplish these tasks.

Tasks to Help You Punish the Injurer

Punishing involves two steps: First, you apprise the offender that she broke a rule and hurt you; and second, you take action that strips choices from her. For a time, at least, her choices will be put aside for yours. To let her know that she committed an unforgivable injury, one of the better methods might be to condemn her openly for hurting you. This first exercise is an important one and should be done with determination and preparation.

Exercise 1: The Condemnation Exercise

This exercise assumes that your injurer is willing to sit down with you and listen to your experience of being harmed. A willing participant is usually motivated to reaffirm your relationship. An unwilling offender usually has no interest in continuing a relationship with you and so will not participate. The condemnation exercise culminates in a face-to-face meeting when you set the terms for punishing the offender. If it is to be a successful exercise, it has to be meticulously planned. There are four steps to the planning. Complete each one carefully.

Step 1: Tell the person who harmed you that you would like to set a time aside to talk about the injury. Make a specific appointment time, even if you are living with the offender. (You might determine if you want a counselor to sit in with you.) Warn the injurer that you intend to say things that will seem to be condemning. This way she can choose to attend or not. There will be no surprises.

Step 2: Prepare for the meeting. Write down what you will say and how you will respond if the injurer denies the injury or walks out, for example. The purpose is to make the offender understand the gravity of her behavior and its permanent effects on you. Plan to tell her about these four points:

1. The nature of the moral rule that was broken.
2. The level of responsibility you assign to her for her role in the injury.
3. The beliefs that were assaulted in the wake of the injury.
4. The appropriate resources you would like to take away from the offender so that you believe the scale is balanced once again.

As you prepare these four points you might want to role-play what you will say. For example:

1. You refused to protect me from my brother when he was violent. I am not wrong to have expected that my mother would protect me from harm.
2. You probably did not intend for me to be abused, but many times when you left the house and my brother was angry, you could have foreseen that he would probably hurt me.
3. Because you failed to protect me, I have never been able to feel safe, even in my close relationships; and because you failed to protect me, I still look for protective relationships. It is not other people's duty to keep me from harm, but I continue to put that burden on others. Therefore, I cannot believe in protection, but I still seek it. These are the beliefs your behavior damaged.
4. This is what I want from you: I want you to acknowledge that you failed to protect me. I want you to apologize. I want for one month to tell you when I think I need protection from something that threatens me. Then I want you to tell me any ideas you have about the threatening situation and methods I can use to resolve it. Finally, I want you to call my brother and tell him he was wrong to hurt me.

These are examples only. Try to decide for your situation how you can effectively impose your expectations on the harmer. In a sense, she will be the object of your choices for a time.

Step 3: Set the time frame for punishment. Decide ahead how long the punishment will last. (A year? Six months? One month?) Will you be willing to negotiate the time frame, or is it fixed?

Step 4: Conduct the condemnation meeting along the following lines:

1. Set the time for the meeting, including the starting time and the ending time, and where it is to be. Decide whether to invite a friend or counselor.
2. Decide the rules beforehand. You will probably want to talk without interruption so that the offender does not offer up justifications or excuses. Make this rule clear before you start the condemnation meeting.
3. Begin the meeting. Cite the four factors of the injury you developed in your preparation (i.e., the moral rule broken, the level of responsibility, the larger injury to beliefs, and the punishment you want to impose). State them as clearly as you can. Use notes if you need to.
4. Ask the offender if she will do two things: Will she apologize for hurting you? Will she promise to comply with the punishment? Be prepared if she tries to negotiate the punishment to her advantage. Decide beforehand how you will respond.

As you can tell, the condemnation meeting could be filled with painful and powerful feelings. It is probably unwise to try it until you have your anger in check. Another option is to put a counselor in the place of your injurer and role-play the condemnation meeting instead. Then you can discuss your responses afterward. (You might also want to do this in preparation for the actual meeting.) Punishment without condemnation is ineffective, as is condemnation without punishment. To condemn and punish effectively, though, you must make sure your extreme emotions are under control. Otherwise, any rage you express may be confused with the terms of punishment you are attempting to set.

Mock Punishment

For adults who were injured as children, maturity often brings with it a new awareness that the injurious actions of a parent were wrong. By the time this conclusion is drawn, however, the offending parent may be dead. Mock punishment is applied when the harmer is not available, as in the case when a parent is dead or an ex-spouse has left the area (or is unwilling to communicate).

The object of mock punishment is for the wounded person, in her imagination, to impose her will on her offender's. As actual punishment does, mock punishment should be designed to include a condemnation. But where no offender is present, there can be no demands on her resources or any imposition on her choices. If this is your situation, try one of these exercises:

Exercise 2: Mock Punishment

If it were possible to make your offender comply with your wishes against her will, how might you accomplish it? Here are three ideas:

1. Imagine you could make the offender sit in a chair and listen to you without talking back or responding to you in any way. Imagine your condemnation. What accusations would you make? What beliefs did she take from you?

2. You are able to put your offender in a prison cell for as long as you would like. How long would the

imprisonment last? What would you say if you could communicate with her through the cell bars?
3. Ask a friend or counselor to play the role of your injurer. Make your demands known through role-playing.

If you are reluctant to think of an appropriate punishment for your harmer, try this exercise:

Exercise 3: Punishment by Proxy

Identify several of your close friends who know your circumstances. Explain to them that you are trying to think of imaginary ways to punish your absent offender. Ask each person for one or two ideas she may have to accomplish this.

1. Select the punishments you are comfortable with and play them out in your imagination or role-play them with someone who is willing to participate.
2. Invite two or three of your closest friends to discuss the situation. Using the list your friends provided, talk about each option. Start out with ways you would deliver the mock punishment. Have your friend contribute to your ideas. Role-play the punishments if you're comfortable doing so. If not, embellish the punishments in your imagination until you think you have exhausted the options.

Mock punishments must be done in the imagination. If you do not think it is necessary to punish your harmer, take an inventory of your current personal life to make sure you are not punishing other people instead. (It's not uncommon for the injured to take their need to punish the injurer out on innocent people.) This can be an unintentional side effect of personal injury. Direct confrontation with the injurer in the form of mock punishment may be a far better alternative than punishing the wrong person or persons subconsciously.

When punishment is not possible or when you have punished your offender all you can but it has not had the effect you had hoped for, your remaining option is to load the scales—take purposeful action to restock your depleted resources. The resources you put back on your side of the scale are more than likely not those that were taken away from you. People who try, for example, to take on a new lover to offset the loss of a spouse (and to instill jealousy) often find that it does not work. The resource lost was the belief one held about marriage or fidelity, perhaps. A new sex partner does not restore that loss. Something else, therefore, must.

The best method of restoring resources is for a wounded person to use her own wound as a source of strength. She can turn it into an advantage if she is creative enough to do so. If that is not possible, she can gain advantage in other ways.

If you have been adding to your gift list (chapter 11), you are already aware of the paradoxical gifts you have acquired as a result of being injured. You may, by this time, have a lengthy list of re-kindled values, new friends or acquaintances, and unexpected kind-nesses that have flowed from your experience. Most of these gifts may have come your way through no effort of your own. Now is the time to go out seeking new resources. What can you give to yourself to bring your resources back into parity?

The following exercises can be framed as gifts to yourself. When you have received enough, you will be able to give the gift of freedom to your injurer.

Exercise 4: New Skills Exercise

Usually, people harbor ideas about some new skills they would like to have but have feared they could not learn. Now is the time to take a risk.

Think of a skill you wish you had. (Needlepoint, speaking Spanish, auto mechanics, photography, driving a car, flying, tennis, carpentry, playing the piano, quilting, and public speaking are just a few.) Look through your telephone book for clubs or service organizations or community colleges where you might take lessons. Ask friends if they might know someone who could teach you. Call your local library for help. If you live in a more isolated area, ask your clergyman or a local community group leader for people they may know who can teach you this skill. If you cannot come up with ideas, look over your diversions list (chapter 10). Are there diversions you have tried but failed to pursue because you did not have the skills you needed?

Acquiring new skills often makes people more versatile and more interesting. Sometimes when you learn new skills, you also make new friends.

Exercise 5: The Friends Exercise

True friends are difficult to come by, yet they are often a person's best resource in both good and bad times. It is easy for people to let old friendships slip away or simply not to make new friends because of busy schedules or other priorities. It is also possible to lose friends during unforgivable injuries, especially in the wake of divorces. Since friendships are powerful resources, it may be time for you to strengthen an old friendship or begin a new one.

How does a person make a new friend? More to the point, what holds a friendship together? The answers are probably similar to the answer you might give about a love relationship. At the heart of either is truthfulness, emotional support, respect, loyalty, and a willingness to listen, talk, and "be in your friend's corner" should difficulties arise. With these ideas in mind, try the following:

1. Select a place where you might have a chance to meet people who have interests similar to yours.
2. Select a time to go to this place. Then make yourself go there.
3. If you meet someone who interests you, attempt to interact as you might with a friend. Be who you really are.

Be honest. You have nothing to lose. Say what you really think (if it is appropriate!). Listen carefully to determine if you like this person and might have things to share with each other. Start slowly. Remember that you are not only a person recovering from being hurt; tell the other person something about yourself apart from the forgiving process. Details about painful experiences may frighten people away.

4. If you like this person, make arrangements to do something pleasant together, like seeing a movie.

5. *Remember, you are not looking for a replacement* for the person who harmed you, or for a counselor, but for a friend. This should make the experience more pleasurable and easier to do because you have nothing to lose if you find you do not have enough interests and similarities to sustain a good friendship.

If you have let important old friendships slip away, find a way to make contact with these people. Explain honestly the reasons you are reaching out to them. Determine this time that you will try harder to maintain these friendships over time, even after you have completely forgiven and moved ahead with your life. Friends are always a source of strength.

To make your own pain work to your advantage, you can turn away from it and give your understanding of it to another person. Understanding pain becomes a personal resource after it is used to the good of someone else in need. Now is the time to turn away from your own problems and begin to focus on those someone else is experiencing. There are plenty of people in any community who are in trouble and in pain. Many of them could use the attention and caring of another individual. Make the choice to get beyond your troubles and move forward by helping others.

Exercise 6: Extending a Hand

The plight and pain of one or another kind of person may have interested you at some time in your life. Here is only a partial list of people who may be in pain: homeless people, abandoned children, lonely people of all ages and kinds, battered and abused people of all sorts, people who are away from their homes against their wishes, terminally ill people, teenage parents without support, people in prisons, and many others.

If any of the kinds of people on the list (or others) tug at your heart and make you want to reach out to them, now may be the time to do it.

1. If you have a United Way or Volunteer Services Bureau in your community, start by calling them. Tell them you would like to volunteer some of your time to help others. They will set up a time to talk with you. Follow through.
2. Look in your yellow pages under "Social Service Organizations." Many of these organizations use the help of volunteers. Try calling one or several of these agencies.
3. Your church or synagogue may have a formal or informal network of people who help the elderly or shut-in or hospitalized members. This may be a place to start.
4. Almost all hospitals use volunteers. Try contacting one of them.

If none of the above options is available where you live, there must be people in your community who have special needs. Is there a way you can help? Could you, for example, drive people to appointments or pick up groceries for them? Could you sit with an elderly or disabled person or child while the caretaker leaves the house for a breather? Could you paint, repair, or fix something for a person who cannot?

Exercise 7: Joining a Support Group

Helping others who have experienced painful situations unlike your own is an important mechanism for turning pain into an asset. Another method is to help people who have been injured in the same way you have. Self-help groups are reported to be immensely helpful to harmed people of all kinds. In these groups, you both give and receive help. Here is a brief list of existing self-help organizations.

For Parents Whose Children Have Died
Parents of Murdered Children
Compassionate Friends

For Partners of Bisexuals
Straight Partners

For People for Whom Sexual Issues Have Been Painful
Parents and Friends of Lesbians and Gays
Sexaholics Anonymous

For People with Chemical Dependencies and Their Families
Alcoholics Anonymous
Al-Anon
Narcotics Anonymous
Women for Sobriety
Al-Ateen
Al-Atot

For People Who Have Harmed Their Children or Been Harmed by Parents
Child Abuse—Parents Anonymous
Teens Together

For People Who Have Been Sexually Abused or Who Have Sexually Abused Their Children
Parents United
Daughters and Sons United

Other self-help groups are described in *The Self-Help Source-book: Finding and Forming Mutual Aid Self-Help Groups*,[1] which is probably available in your library reference section.

Go to several meetings of the group that best fits your situation. While you are sure to be helped, try to focus on other people's problems, too. You might be immensely helpful to another person with your shared insights and stories. You have nothing to lose in trying this. (If you do not find a group to be helpful, by no means should you feel you must continue to attend meetings. Another kind of group might work better for you. Make sure, though, that you atttend enough meetings to be able to judge whether a group matches your needs or not.)

If you find that your community does not have a group that fits your situation, could you start your own group? This takes time, energy, and commitment, but it can be accomplished. If starting groups is not possible, tell your clergy or another community person of your willingness to help someone who has experienced a situation similar to yours. Someone familiar with your community might be able to provide a linkage for you.

Paradoxically, many beautiful works of art, poetry, and prose have germinated from great pain. While most people lack the talent to produce great art, many can produce good art. Try this exercise:

Exercise 8: Creating Something Beautiful

Look over your journal, especially your gift list. If you are an artist, try to draw, paint, or sculpt a work that represents the gifts you have received because of your unforgivable wound. If you are a writer or poet, write something that expresses the beauty of the benefits you have taken from having been hurt. If you are a seamstress or weaver, create a piece that expresses your gratitude for the gifts of the injury. If you are a musician, write a song reflecting the good that has come from your suffering.

A final exercise in this phase of forgiving applies where people have concluded that they were as much to blame as their injurer. Both were wrong, and both could have foreseen that their behavior might result in irreparable harm. If this is your conclusion, try the next exercise.

Exercise 9: The Thank-You Note

Take out some stationery and write a thank-you note to the person who hurt you. Let it come naturally. Think of as many gifts your injurer gave you as you can. These should be not only material gifts but also gifts of caring or generosity or other intangible sources of pleasure or gratitude you remember. Thank the injurer for the gifts that have come your way as a result of the injury as well. When you are done, tuck the letter away somewhere. Sometime you may choose to mail it.

The phase of forgiving in which you bring the scales back into balance is a critical one. It is critical because forgiveness comes from strength, not weakness. To forgive, you must believe that you are as strong, as endowed with resources, or as blameworthy as the person who hurt you. Punishing, mock-punishing, and loading the scales together accomplish this objective. Once you are strong, you have only one more task ahead: to choose to forgive.

CHAPTER 14

Tools for Choosing to Forgive

> Only the brave know how to forgive. . . . A coward never forgave; it is not in his nature.
>
> LAURENCE STERNE

U nforgivable injuries leave an unexpected and precious gift in their wake—the potential of freedom to start life over again. Freedom, for the injured, however, remains only a potential until they are able to free their injurers. The injured must choose to set their injurers free. In doing so, they also set themselves free.

When you choose to forgive, you tear up all outstanding IOUs. Your offender owes you nothing more. You choose to sever your identity from that of your injurer. You choose to move forward with your life and not dwell on the past. If you and your harmer happen to move forward together, you set a new course for a reaffirmed relationship and must carve out new beliefs, hopes, and dreams for yourselves.

The barriers to choosing to forgive reflect the fear of loss—the loss of an identity, loss of specialness, loss of face, and loss of the last shred of attachment and control you believe you have over your offender. People may falsely believe that if they hold out for all debts to be paid off, they retain power over those who still owe them something, or at least retain their moral "correctness." The problem is that, in most cases, the injurer believes no debt is owed, and if both parties do not agree that a debt is owed, any power behind demands that a person pay off the debt is only an illusion. To be able to choose to forgive, a wounded person must relinquish any remaining illusions that he can require the injurer to pay off some debt.

The first nine exercises prepare for the choice to forgive. They are designed to help you give up any lingering ideas you may have about your control over your injurer or your need to rely on him for your identity. (Remember, he probably does not know that you believe you have any remaining control over him.) Try one or more of the following exercises to help you sever the bonds:

Exercise 1: Erasing the Labels

To choose to forgive you must be free from defining yourself in any way in relation to the unforgivable situation you have experienced. To accomplish this, try one of the following:

Write down any term you have used to define yourself in relation to your offender. Examples may be "abused," "dumpee," "ex-wife," "victim," "betrayed ———," "cuckold," "codependent," or any other. After completing the list, check for any of these labels you still are using in conversation.

Make a contract with the following terms:

For one week you will:

1. Not use any of the labels you wrote down (in any social conversation).
2. Refer to yourself only in the context of other aspects of

who you are (your interests, hobbies, family, friends or work, for example).
3. Try to change the subject politely if people inquire about the unforgivable situation and tell them the reason for your behavior.

If you succeed for the week, try the same exercise for another week.

Exercise 2: "You Don't Owe Me"

With your counselor or a friend (or an empty chair or a picture of your injurer), practice saying this:

"You don't owe me anything anymore. I don't want you to repay me. You are free."

Do *not* do this until you feel that you can mean it.

If you cannot bring yourself to say the words in exercise 2, answer this: What do you still believe the injurer owes you? If you believe he owes you an apology or a "thank you," try the next exercise.

Exercise 3: Thanking Yourself

Even though you are strong now and poised to move forward, you may still harbor the wish that the person who hurt you had taken the time to apologize or to say "thank you" for all that you did over the years. When relationships rupture, people rarely take time to express gratitude for the time, support, and caring they have given each other. You may still be waiting to hear a "thank you" from your injurer. In all likelihood, though, it will not come.

On a piece of stationery, write a thank-you note to yourself as though it had been written by your injurer. Take time to include any important contribution you feel you made. When you are ready, have your friend or counselor read the letter to you, thanking you one by one for each of the things you listed.

For example, the friend might say directly to you, "Thank you for giving me moral support when I was a student. I don't know if I could have graduated without your help."

In return, say, "You're welcome. I wanted to help you and was proud when you graduated." Respond with "You're welcome" to each thing you are thanked for.

This can be a powerful experience. When you have finished, talk about your feelings.

With love comes a special bond and a history that is yours alone. Forgiving does not undo your history together or invalidate the fact that you have loved. Forgiving acknowledges that you are moving ahead independently but does not mean that you were never special to the person who hurt you. To reaffirm and validate your special history with the injurer, try the following:

Exercise 4: The Scrapbook

This exercise may take some time. It actually could be started at almost any time during the forgiving process. If you have not begun a similar inventory, now is the time to chronicle your history with your injurer.

Go back through letters, photographs, mementos, and other special sentimental things you have collected over the course of your relationship with the person who hurt you. If you already have albums and scrapbooks of your relationship, gather up the items that remain uncataloged (like pictures, postcards, etc.) and spend time placing these objects into your album. If you have never organized a special album about your history with this person, begin to do it now. You might put photographs in order from the begin-

224 / Forgiving the Unforgivable

ning of your relationship until it ruptured, or you may organize it in a different way.

Look at each picture. Read the letters. Let your feelings come out.

When you have cataloged everything, keep the album around for a while. Study it when you have a moment. When you are ready, put it away, out of sight. (You can always get it out again. But for now, the album is finished.) It is time to look ahead.

Exercise 5: The Balloon Exercise

Make a list of lingering debts you still feel your injurer owes you (or "wants" that you wish you could have from him). By now, this list should be quite short, but if you still harbor any idea that he owes you something, write it down.

Go to a party store and buy some helium-filled balloons. On each write the items on your "debt list" with a magic marker.

If you have a spot where you are reminded of your injurer, go there with your balloons. Imagine that the balloons with the debts written on them are the last remaining connections you have with your injurer. Think about the details of his face. Remember the debts he will never repay.

When you are ready, release your hold on the balloons one by one. Imagine you are relinquishing the last threads that connect you to the injurer as you watch the balloons rise. Grieve if you need to; but remember, you have freed your harmer.

Exercise 6: The IOU Exercise

Write out an imaginary IOU. On it, list every debt you believe the offender still owes you. Study the list. Will he ever repay you? *Can* he ever repay you?

When you are ready, and really *mean* it, shred the IOU.
He now owes you nothing on the list. The debt is forgiven.

Forgiving can increase responsibilities. If you decide you have no one except yourself to hold accountable for the quality of your life, you accept responsibility for any future difficulties you may encounter. You will need to solve your own problems from now on (or seek help from someone other than your injurer to solve them). This, for many people, is a new responsibility.

Forgiving can also impose difficult expectations on you where your injurer is concerned (e.g., that you resume talking with your brothers and sisters or accept a child's spouse of whom you disapprove). When you anticipate some of the changes you may still have to make to meet these new responsibilities, you may resent your injurer all over again. (After all, you have changed enough because of the injury. That it should again force you to take on new responsibilities might be the final resentment that stands in the way of forgiving.)

If you have not identified these new responsibilities, try this exercise:

Exercise 7: "If I forgave you, I'd have to _____*."*

> Try to think of the most important realms of your life (e.g., work, family, clubs, etc.). Considering these realms, try to imagine what, if any, new responsibilities you might have to take on if you forgave your injurer. Are they responsibilities you can handle, and is your forgiving important enough to take them on anyhow?

Aside from new responsibilities, you might fear a loss of face if you choose to forgive. Others who have supported you throughout the entire forgiving process may still want you to hold out for repayment or encourage you to harbor anger. This is natural, because friends who witness your struggle with pain become an integral part of it. They may fear that if you choose to forgive, you are acknowledging that you are to blame rather than your injurer. If this is the case, you must reassure your supporters that choosing to forgive has nothing to do with blame. Instead, tell supporters that forgiving empowers because it signals that you are now so strong, you need nothing from the offender. The strong can let go. If you find that your friends or supporters will not understand your choice to forgive, try this exercise:

Exercise 8: "If I forgave, my friends would _____.*"*

> Identify the major people who have given you support over the course of forgiving. Try to imagine what each might say if you revealed you wanted to forgive your injurer.
>
> Now identify others who have been aware of your situation, particularly family members. What might each of them say if you said you have forgiven your harmer?
>
> Is any of these responses important enough to prevent you from moving ahead toward the choice to forgive?

You might also harbor the deep fear that if you forgive, you must really believe that you are responsible for the injury. If you are stuck with this lingering misconception, try this exercise:

Exercise 9: "You're still to blame, but I want nothing from you."

> Think of the injurer again. Then say this sentence,

> *"You're still to blame, but I no longer want* ——— *from you."*

The missing word might be love, money, nurturing, support, telephone calls, apologies, thank-yous, promises, respect, or any number of other old expectations.

The nine preparatory tasks are designed to lead you to a position of strength from which you can say aloud, "I forgive you." The four fears—fear of invalidating one's history, fear of new responsibilities, fear of loss of face, and fear of losing one's identity—have now been overcome. The only task remaining is to choose to say, "I forgive you." When you choose this, you choose to look toward the future from now on.

Exercise 10: Saying "I Forgive You"

Ask a friend or your counselor to sit in a chair facing you. Imagine once again that this is the person who hurt you and that after today you will be free of all your old relationship.

When you are ready, begin by saying, "———, I forgive you. What you did wounded me deeply. That does not mean that we haven't loved each other. We have. Forgiving you means that I no longer want anything from you. You are free to go on your way, as I am free to go on mine. You are forgiven, and we are free."

Choosing to forgive is the act of a brave person, one who has struggled against the deepest of pain brought about by an intimate injurer. When you have forgiven, you have accomplished one of the most difficult tasks of living. Your future is now yours. You are free to make it what you can.

CHAPTER **15**

Reflections on the New Self

> Great grief . . . transforms the wretched.
> VICTOR HUGO

W hen you have forgiven the unforgivable, you have been transformed. The person who hurt you no longer poisons your heart. Whether you have decided that you cannot control life's events or whether you now believe that there is universal but inscrutable orderliness to events—even awful ones—you are at peace. Your new beliefs about justice and control fit with your new ideas about yourself, others, and injury. No injury could ever again be driven so deeply into your heart as to be called "unforgivable." The worst is over.

This does not mean that your new set of beliefs will not be tested; it will. It does not mean that you will never be hurt again; you will. But your new beliefs will pull you through as you embark on the next phase of your life. Your new beliefs, when tested, will not crumble apart under the weight of an injury. They are too finely woven together for weight to rip apart; probably nothing will ever seem to be unforgivable again.

The next phase of your life will be a journey forward on a new course. Before you go, it might be productive to pause and write down what you believe at this moment. You have succeeded at one of life's most difficult processes. If you stumble or falter, you may want to look back again at all the work you have done and the changes you have gone through. A statement about who you are right now might anchor you in future times of confusion or turmoil.

Now is the time to celebrate your accomplishments. Now is a time to respect yourself for your hard work and your resolute refusal to be destroyed or embittered.

The last entry in your notebook should be a statement of your forgiveness principle. Now that you have come to accept personal harm as a part of living, a written statement about forgiveness might help to remind you of your new beliefs and the boundaries you will set to control any injuries in the future.

Final Exercise: The Forgiveness Principle

Write a statement in your forgiveness journal about your new philosophy for the future if harm should come your way again. Here is a suggestion:

I know that I cannot prevent harm from coming my way. It is the rare person who escapes being injured by a person she loves. I will remove myself from harm's way when I can; but in the future I will know that injuries happen to everyone. Some of them I will be able to control. Some I will not. Knowing this, I am free. Forgiving will never again be so difficult.

When you have forgiven the unforgivable, you have accomplished what many others have not been able to do. Take pride in yourself as you start your new life.

PART IV

The Need to Forgive

16

The Need to Forgive

It is human nature to hate those whom you have injured.

TACITUS, *Agricola*

To forgive someone you have loved—or to be forgiven by someone you have loved and then hurt—may be more than a desire. Forgiving may be a need. I emphasize "may" because needs cross over the barriers of language, culture, and politics to the very heart of what makes us people. Desires are anchored in what people want or covet; needs are anchored in what is essential. If forgiveness is a human need, it is because it is essential to people's survival or capacity to thrive.

Water is a need driven by thirst. Without water, people die. Food is a need driven by hunger. The hungry person is dominated by cravings to fill an empty belly. The unforgiving or unforgiven person may, like a person with a parched tongue, need forgiveness not for physical survival but for survival more intangible. Essential physical needs left unmet result in physical death. Essential emotional needs left unmet might result in an emotional denouement—the shriveling of the capacity to love and be loved, to trust and be trusted. Human beings without these capacities might think themselves as "dead" as those who are truly so.

Unresolved injuries between strangers may pass away with time. Unforgiven injuries between people who have loved each other do not. Time and remoteness cannot erase unforgivable injuries. All too many people live far away from the ones they have loved, yearning to hear the words "I'm sorry" or "I forgive you." If these words are never spoken, the heart can simply begin a long wait while the slow process of its withering in unwatered moral ground, as parched as a dry tongue, takes hold and destroys its victim.

If forgiveness between intimate people who violate each other's moral expectations is truly a need and not simply a desire, what is the basis for the need? Why, for example, would an old, dying man still struggle to forgive his elderly wife for an indiscretion she engaged in years before? Why would old friends who parted in hatred and betrayal call each other years later to try to make amends? In a way, the philosopher Immanuel Kant had an answer for this. He called this need to reconcile the unresolved the "moral law within," the ideal that human beings have an "inner sensitivity about the way things ought to be."[1] Normal, morally developed people* want to do right. We do not like to experience the feelings of guilt that follow our betrayal of a person we have loved. People yearn for peacefulness with, and good feelings toward, other people. If the nightmarish guilt associated with justifiable assaults on enemies during warfare awakens many a soldier in the night, even more unsettling are the guilt and pain that persist in the wake of an unforgivable, intimate injury. It is too difficult to go through life feeling "not right" about enemies, let alone someone you have borne, married, raised, or held in your arms and cried with.

---

* People who suffer various forms of mental illness may not have the capacity to know right from wrong. Guilt may also be missing among people with various personality disorders.

We have an inner need to come to the end of our lives with a clear conscience and a peaceful heart. Unforgivable injuries that are left unforgiven thwart this need. Without forgiveness, time and circumstance may quiet the voices of guilt or sorrow that follow unforgivable injuries, but remoteness will not silence these feelings totally. Forgiveness does.

Needs and Survival

The problem with forgiveness being a need is this: The need to forgive or be forgiven may no longer be compatible with, or necessary to, human survival. If everyone in an Eskimo village fifty years ago was hungry and the village hunters gathered to kill a walrus, the walrus's death accomplished two things. Each individual's need for food was met, and the survival of the village was assured because the hunters, cooks, and medicine men were well fed. Individual needs and community survival were "in synch" with one another. Where people were dependent on one another, individual needs and group survival were mutually supportive concepts. When one was met, the other was more likely guaranteed.

Forgiveness of an errant community member in all likelihood enhanced the chances for survival of the entire community. Today the need to forgive may be only a remnant of the individual's capacity to feel guilt and contrition for mistreating another individual. Interpersonal forgiveness may have no collective dividends. In fact, survival in business, school, or on the job now depends on individual accomplishment and competitive edge more than on mutual dependency and cooperation. The need to forgive might collide directly with the attitudes and skills it takes to succeed in our fiercely competitive society. What now?

What if we, at the end of the twentieth century, are left with the inner need to forgive people we have loved but forgiveness has no larger meaning to the community of people as a whole? What if personal emotional survival and survival on the job or in business have become incompatible notions?

People are expendable. We can find new doctors or lawyers, interior decorators, or even spouses. We no longer need one person to forgive another person to assure the survival of all.

Or do we?

Is Forgiveness Essential to Survival?

What if no one forgave anyone? What might happen in a society in which forgiveness was neither an interpersonal need nor a valued mechanism for reconciling interpersonal problems? Would the very private matter of nonforgiveness affect the public's well-being?

Suppose there were three different societies in which forgiveness did not exist. In these three societies offenders and those they offend are still able to feel the anguish of an unforgivable offense. (In other words, there is still a moral element in people's makeup. Private moral contracts between people are still drawn, and people can still feel guilt and grief, contrition and hatred.) However, in these three societies, forgiveness does not exist. No one values it—not individuals or community groups, churches or therapists. In these societies, people carry their injuries on, but they do this in one of three different ways. In the first society, people must not retaliate or attempt revenge, but they must continue to live in the same community with the offender. In the second society, people act upon their anger and attempt to "get even." In the third society, people move far away from each other, carrying their injuries with them but eliminating any possibility for face-to-face confrontations with each other.

How would societies in which forgiveness does not exist look? Is there any residual link between the ways intimate injuries are reconciled and the ways a society lives, works, and plays?

Society One: Nonforgiveness in Close Proximity

Imagine that two middle-aged parents have an unforgivable falling-out with their young adult daughter. No one retaliates. They do not move away. In their society, people never forgive one another, but they must live in continued proximity to one another. How would these parents and their daughter act? How would their actions and the actions of others affect the community they live in? The broader question is this: How would guilt, rage, sorrow, and contrition play out between people who never forgave each other but who were likely to run into each other if they were not careful?

People who have hurt each other (at least when retaliation is out of the question) have two options: They can approach one another to attempt reconciliation, or they can avoid each other. In this society, approach is not valued or condoned. If a face-to-face reunion happened, it would serve no purpose. So complete avoidance of an injurer or a person one hurt is the only option that makes sense. The problem is, if people live in close proximity, the probability that one person can completely avoid another is unlikely. To avoid each other as completely as possible, people would need to take special precautions to assure that they will not run into each other unexpectedly. How would the parents and their daughter arrange this? Several steps would need to be taken.

First, the parents and daughter sort through all the activities they have engaged in together. One by one, they systematically avoid places where they have previously encountered one another. The first week after the unforgivable injury, they stop going to church. Next, they drop out of the company bowling league and the fireman's club. When spring comes, all three quit playing softball on the neighborhood tavern team. The mother stops volunteering at the community hospital because her daughter is a nurse there. After a while, all of the places where they were sure to have seen each other are avoided. With that, the likelihood of a face-to-face confrontation is diminished considerably. There are still worries, however. What if they were to join other clubs or churches? How could each know the other would not join the same ones?

To assure no new potential confrontations, the parents and daughter begin to send out "scouts." They ask their friends to attend events, keeping a sharp eye out for the other party. If the scouts report back that the other is not participating, the offended or offender might try out some new activity or club. When the scouts begin to tire of their duty, the parents and daughter begin to drive past the parking lots when the other might be attending an activity to see if the other's car is in the lot. If it is, then the activity will be avoided in the future. In addition, before going to any social event, each party calls the host or club chairperson to make sure the other is not included in the guest or membership list.

At holiday time, the family and friends of the family are asked to pick sides. Some choose the parents; others, the daughter. No one who goes to one home is invited to the other and vice versa. These "allies" are seen as enemies to the other from then on.

On a routine day-to-day basis, the parents and daughter travel about with great caution, trying assiduously to avoid common streets they might take to the grocery store or mall. If they *must* come in contact, they steel themselves against one another. They avoid eye contact; they attempt to speak, if they meet, through third parties. Their lives, little by little, come to be lived in rigid, predictable patterns. Their activities are cordoned off, and they are more and more cautious. Finally, they find themselves unwilling to go out for fear of an unpleasant, unpredicted run-in. They, in effect, live the lives of willing prisoners.

Now, imagine a whole community engaging in similar avoidance strategies. Friends plan their days around not seeing each other. Ex-spouses hire private detectives to help them find ways to avoid confrontations. People who have been unforgivably wounded by one person but who have hurt someone else must try to avoid both. Life driven by avoidance is complex. Imagine a life planned around avoiding more than one person! The obvious result of nonforgiveness in this hypothetical society is that, after a while, most people would become so tired of avoiding others that they might just stay home. Avoidance, taken to its extreme, is isolation.

An isolated society seems the conceivable end product of a nonforgiving society in which people must live close together. The isolation would likely be physical, but it might be psychological in the form of people taking on rigid defenses should they see one another unexpectedly.

Are there any ways that this particular nonforgiving society could break through individual isolation? Possibly, but it would be difficult.

One way for injurers and injured not to have their lives controlled by their unforgiven injuries might be for them to travel about incognito. People might wear masks or have plastic surgery. Then they could go unrecognized and not need to avoid each other. If people still wanted the company of others so that they were not so individually isolated, they could form special clubs. Each club would comprise people who had never harmed or been harmed by anyone else in the group. Other common interests or characteristics among members might be difficult to find, but at least people could meet for coffee. Meeting times could be published or posted so that all affected parties could stay clear of the club while it met. (Of course, as soon as the next club member unforgivably wounded another member, the two participants would have to be expelled, and so on, until the club would have to break up.) In this hypothetical society, it becomes clear that interpersonal nonforgiveness would indeed affect the larger community. It would affect clubs, churches, people's mobility, the workplace, and ultimately, the very idea of life without constraints.

The fluid comings and goings of people who are not defined or governed by their injuries would give way to caution and rigidity. People would come to live lives where movement would be constrained, families and friends separated, and spontaneity nearly impossible. This is how individual nonforgiveness could spill over onto others and affect the general well-being of a society, at least hypothetically. If we look hard enough, we might see some of this happening now, in the nonhypothetical. First, though, consider the second society: What if no one moved away but everyone involved in an unforgivable injury was encouraged to seek revenge?

Society Two: Retaliation in Kind

What if interpersonal retaliation were the societally sanctioned response to unforgivable injuries? In hypothetical Society Two, where injured and injurers continue to live in close proximity, revenge and retaliation are accepted. Harm is met with equal harm. Forms of repayment for injury are not adjudicated in the courtroom or mediated by an uninvolved party; instead, repayment for injury may take any form the offender and offended decide it should take. What would happen between the parents and their young adult daughter in a society like this? How might their actions affect the community?

The offense between the two parties started when the daughter borrowed a great deal of money from the parents and then refused to repay them. She stopped answering the phone when they called. She stopped going to visit them. She simply told her parents she had no intention of paying them back. With that, she shattered their dreams of a retirement condo in Arizona, their view of themselves as having raised a nice person as their daughter, and their assumption that their daughter loved them and their bond held mutuality and trust. In Society Two, what would the parents do next? Since forgiveness in Society Two is out of the question, as it was in Society One, and since people attack rather than avoid here, the simple answer is that the parent would immediately retaliate. The form of the retaliation is up to the parents.

First, they decide to write the daughter a note telling her she has been cut out of their will. She shoots a letter back that they will no longer, or ever again, be able to visit her son, their only grandchild. Next, they go to her house and steal her car, quickly selling it to a middleman who delivers it to a distant town. They view the money as partial repayment of the loan. The daughter then steals her mother's favorite expensive cut glass and puts it away in a safe. With each action and reaction, the ante goes up, and so does the degree of violence and hatred between the parties. Finally, physical harm is done. Someone is hospitalized. Still the retaliation does not stop. It cannot totally stop in Society Two. People may take "breathers," but they must live in close proximity and try to "get even" with those who hurt them.

Since retaliation is ordinarily a symmetrical interaction—that is, since one injurious action elicits an equally or slightly more harmful reaction—retaliation ordinarily spirals until one or both parties are nearly destroyed. When any two parties are bent on destruction, there is bound to be some impact on the community they live in. What would life be like if everyone retaliated against those who unforgivably wounded them? Here is one scenario:

At night, sleep in most neighborhoods is disrupted several times during the course of the evening with the sirens of ambulances racing to take assault victims to the hospitals. The sounds of breaking windows and screams punctuate the night air. Fire engines race from one burning home to the next as betrayed spouses attempt to destroy whatever is left of the other's assets. In the grocery store, fights break out between ex-friends who happen to run into each other in the frozen-food aisle.

A person's days are filled with making plans to get back at people. Productivity is at a near standstill. Life without forgiveness, if retaliation were the norm, would be dreadful and threatening. There would be two themes: planning your strategy for harming your offender and planning your strategy for protecting yourself against retaliation. Soon the laws of the jungle would prevail. The cagiest, meanest, and, perhaps, fittest, would survive. The weaker would falter. Like the nonretaliators in Society One, though, every person would be on his own. Isolation would predominate, but its source would be different. A community of independent warriors who retaliate with impunity would be as filled with isolates as a community of those who avoid confrontation. Warriors must survive on their craftiness, not only their ability to avoid other people.

In Society One, people would grow tired of avoiding each other. In Society Two, people would become isolated in order to simply survive. Would there be any way out of personal isolation in Society Two? Perhaps. The way out, however, might result in even larger-scale violence. The weaker, for example, could form gangs. They could pool their money to buy larger or more deadly weapons. They could take action against each other's injurers as well as their own. Mutual dependency would revolve around individual strategies for harming offenders or for protecting individuals against retaliation. Taken to the extreme, roving gangs of offenders and offended people could dominate the life of Society Two. Revenge might become big business, and the connectedness between people would generate out of mutual needs for protection or power.

In this nonforgiving, retaliatory society, it is clear that individuals who retaliate against unforgivable injuries permeate the community with broad violence. Broad violence would, in all likelihood, bring community life to a standstill through either complete destruction or domination of the very strong over the weak. Personal nonforgiveness and societal well-being are more clearly connected in this scenario; no society could exist for long where retaliation was the sanctioned method of resolving intimate injuries. No society where forgiveness was totally supplanted with approved retaliation could endure. Isolation would give way to brutality; brutality, to broad destruction. Society Two is one that could not long survive.

What about the third hypothetical nonforgiving society? What would happen if people did not avoid those involved in their injuries but did not attempt to "get even," either? What if people simply left one another, never to be seen again?

Society Three: Escape, Remoteness, and Time

In Society Three, people who are harmed in unforgivable injuries do not fight back, and they do not remain in close proximity and attempt to dodge each other. Instead, they simply leave. They do not seek each other out ever again, and they do not attempt to maintain any ties. They let escape be their method to resolve pain and time be their healer. What could be wrong with this? It is much like our own society. At least in this hypothetical situation people are not burning each other's houses down or hiding in their family rooms at night for fear of unwanted confrontation. People's lives go forward. They make new acquaintances. They start their lives over. How could this form of nonforgiveness have an impact on the larger community or on society as a whole?

In Society Three, the parents go to their adult daughter's house and demand that she repay the loan. They are heartbroken, and while she feels bad, she sees no obligation to comply with their demand.

Clearly, one of the parties must move away to prevent this unforgivable injury from affecting anyone else. The parents will not forgive; the daughter will not apologize or make good on the debt. In Society Three, the only societally approved resolution to this situation is that one party leave. Since the daughter is less settled than her parents and not a homeowner, she takes advantage of the resettlement-program dollars (paid for through general tax revenues). She packs her belongings, her child, and herself into a rental truck and moves to a city many miles away, never to be heard from again.

The parents go on about their lives, never uttering their daughter's name. They remove her pictures from the walls. They destroy old report cards, prom dresses, and school yearbooks in a bonfire party, with their friends looking on. Since the resettlement was published in the newspaper, family friends know never to bring up the daughter's name. Fellow workers, their clergyman, and family doctor treat the parents as though the daughter had never been born. She is a nonperson—gone and forgotten.

The daughter, too, goes on with her life. She marries again, but since her new husband understands the process of resettlement, he never asks about her parents. She changes all of the personal documents she can legally change to exclude their names. She destroys all pictures of them. She has her maiden name removed from any printed matter. When her son asks her questions about his grandparents, she tells him that she does not discuss them and that he is not to ask about them again. She does not malign them; she just says nothing. (Or, if she says anything about them, it is only that she engaged in resettlement some years before. This way, people do not ask questions.) Each party is gone to the other. There is no retaliation; there is no avoidance. Life has just gone on, and nonforgiveness continues in the form of unspoken resentment.

This form of interpersonal nonforgiveness seems to have no impact on the broader community. Maybe people do not ask personal questions of one another in Society Three, but what else, if anything, could possibly be affected in such a quiet dissolution of a personal relationship? The answer, if we look closely, is "Plenty."

In a society in which people, once injured, never face each other, the major loss involves one's history. People not only leave their injurers or those they injure; they also leave old friends, their communities, schools, churches, and clubs. They leave connectedness behind them.

What is most lost in Society Three is the continuity of life, the thread of connectedness from generation to generation. Once people are resettled, their family histories, old loyalties, and personal pasts are ripped from their roots. Not only do the resettled lose their histories, but so, too, do those associated with them. The daughter's son has no family history beyond his mother. Her husband knows nothing of her past. If everyone in a nonforgiving society escaped his wounds through physical relocation, society would consist of small bands of drifting settlers searching for new homes until the next injury happened. There could be little room for developing loyalties or friendships. People could barely afford to put down roots. Life would be governed by escape; escape would be dictated by unforgiven wounds.

Could there be a way, in Society Three, for people to develop any friendships? Yes, there could. There would be clubs and teams and volunteer organizations. There would be churches and businesses and government. There simply would be little personal investment in any of them. Once an injury occurred between church members or co-workers, one would again resettle. People could little afford to become too deeply involved in anything. Their "roots" would be their own life story. People's roots would spread, like creeping Charlie roots, just under the ground's surface—easily grown, just as easily ripped up.

In Society Three, like Societies One and Two, the final outcome of nonforgiveness is personal isolation. People would become isolated from one another through avoidance or defensiveness or superficial connectedness. They might live lives of constant, rigid planning or vigilant protectiveness or rootless drifting. Whatever form life in nonforgiving society takes (at least in these three hypothetical situations), one thing is clear: Personal nonforgiveness has a profound impact on society as a whole. The actions of two individuals spill over onto the community and society. Hypothetically, nonforgiveness alienates people from one another; it reduces society to a disjointed collection of individuals for whom harm has come to dominate their very lives. Nonforgiveness, hypothetically, ultimately weakens the fabric of the human community. Each person, with his individual baggage of resentment and sorrow, carries his load alone. Preoccupied with one's own situation, one could barely have energy or time to assist another person. Nonforgiveness leads to self-preoccupation, and preoccupation with the self leads to isolation.

Nonforgiveness in Reality

Does nonforgiveness or any of its hypothetical side effects affect us in our society now? Is there any way of knowing whether cutthroat business practices or divorce rates or increases in violent crimes, for example, could be the last ripple in the ripple effect of nonforgiveness? Probably not. Some, if not most, of the interviewees, however, were acutely and painfully aware that their own experiences of being unable to forgive had washed over not only them but many others. Some people expressed fear that their long inability to forgive their spouses had permanently harmed their children, for example. Others talked about the effects that their inability to forgive had on their associates and friends. In one case, the experience of a nun who was hurt by another sister affected the entire church community. The bitterness of nonforgiveness almost certainly contaminates our communities and our society. We simply do not know how to measure it.

If we were to accept, even minimally, that nonforgiveness could hurt us all, how would we act? What if we treated nonforgiveness like sexually transmitted diseases, each person who carries it having the potential of infecting everyone with whom he comes into intimate (and even other) contact? If we viewed it this way, we would probably create some programs or policies to help stop nonforgiveness in its tracks.

Society Four: The Surrogate Forgiveness Society

What if there were a society in which forgiveness was respected and promoted? What if, in addition to society's provision of social institutions to promote health and education, there were a society that developed social institutions to actively promote forgiveness? In this society, which we will call the Surrogate Forgiveness Society, unreconciled hatred is regarded as lethal as unchecked hepatitis. This being the case, Society Four provides surrogates, or "stand-ins," to help people forgive each other when they are unable to accomplish the task on their own. We return to the derelict daughter from Societies One, Two, and Three.

Our "daughter in debt" continues to live far away from her home. She is in her early forties now and by chance runs into a recent newcomer to town who reports her parents' tragic death in a car accident some years before. She is bothered but detached from feeling any grief.

Her life has been successful by most standards. Her work has taken her to numerous interesting projects. Her son moved away immediately after graduating. She has had many acquaintances and friends. Her marriage has held together. Still, she has felt that something is missing. She feels alone a great deal of the time and does not know why. Soon after her introduction to the newcomer from her hometown, she has a dream in which her parents' shadows appear. A friend, soon after, borrows some money and fails to return it. This betrayal reminds her of the way she treated her parents. One day, she is overwhelmed with the desire to visit her hometown.

After consulting with her husband, the daughter sets out to rekindle the faded memories of her past. She buys a ticket home and flies there. Upon arrival, everything looks entirely different. She rents a car and, with difficulty because there is a freeway now, finds the way to her old neighborhood. She is grateful to see her home still standing. The wonderful elm trees on her street are gone now, leaving the street bare to the sun instead of protected under the lovely green canopy.

The house is small and now painted a different color. She argues with herself whether to try to go inside or not; she decides against it. A child plays in the yard. A blue car is parked in the driveway.

The daughter lingers a while longer and then drives up the street toward her old school. It has been torn down. Her church has given way to an insurance company headquarters. She goes to a phone book to look up names of several old friends. One person's name is there, but she decides not to call. There is one last thing to do.

With great reluctance, she points the car toward the cemetery where her family is buried. She finds her way there with surprising ease. Turning into the cobblestone drive, she spots the family plot just to the left, under what is now a grove of tall box elder. The daughter stops the car and forces herself from the seat. Next to the far headstone, her grandfather's, are two new ones. She knows they are those of her parents. Their names look odd, chiseled into the gray marble. Their names are like so much newspaper print on the op-ed page of her daily paper. They mean nothing to her. They are figures in stone. The daughter heads to the rental car drop-off at the airport and flies home.

For two weeks things go normally; then the dreams begin again. The faces of her parents appear as blurs. There are no details. During the day, this starts to bother her. She begins to wonder how her parents' voices sounded. One day, she imagines she can hear the venetian blinds in her childhood bedroom gently blowing back and forth and clicking, as they did when she was a child, against the windowsill. She dreams one night that she is throwing a ball to her dog, and when she moves her eyes toward the house, she sees her father. This time, she awakens crying.

In Society Four, there are advertisements everywhere for "forgiving services and counseling." Articles are featured every week in most newspapers about old friends who have reunited and forgiven each other. Politicians openly admit on television when they have made mistakes. They often issue public apologies. The more honest a leader is, the more admired he or she is.

Educators teach children ways to say "I'm sorry." Churches offer special classes in "Trading 'Getting Even' for 'Getting Along.' "

The morning she wakes up crying, the daughter decides she must take some action. She puts a call through to her local Call for Help Hot Line. The worker on call listens to her and suggests that she call one of the community's forgiveness centers. She does, and with some trepidation she sets up her first appointment.

Forgiveness centers in Society Four are paid for with state tax funds and staffed with professionals who specialize in the process of forgiveness. There are also volunteer actors on staff who play various roles. Some play the roles of children who were injured by their parents. Some specialize in middle-aged issues of forgiving former friends or lovers. Others play the roles of injurers. Some take special classes in the amending of promise breaking; others, on the hurtfulness of lies. Each is thoroughly trained and understands the phases and nuances of the forgiving process.

When the daughter comes to the agency for her first appointment, she tells the professional coordinator the details of her refusal to pay back her parents' loan. She explains how she moved away and took their only grandchild with her. She tells about her troubling dreams. The professional asks her to return the next week with an assignment completed. How did nonrepayment of the loan actually hurt her parents? What beliefs did they lose? What did they feel when they died?

In the next week, the daughter thinks about her parents and about the condo in Arizona her parents never had because of her and how they lost faith in their own parenting. She reflects on how much they looked forward to being good grandparents and how they died not knowing her. When she finishes her assignment, she feels something toward them for the first time. She feels grief. She knows she destroyed her parents' dreams.

For the next six weeks, the daughter schedules weekly appointments at the forgiveness center. She is introduced to the two volunteers who play the roles of her parents. They are well prepared and seem to understand how her parents must have felt. They are also about the ages of her parents, if they had lived. The first meetings are painful and difficult. The surrogate forgivers—the "parents"—tell her every way she harmed them. They cry. They are angry. They name their lost dreams and blame her squarely for violating a moral agreement they had. After the initial extreme emotions play out and several weeks go by, the daughter asks the surrogate what they want her to do. It is important that she ask them, not they her. They answer that they want her to apologize.

The daughter has rarely apologized, but she desperately wants to now. She seeks out the professional who helps her plan what it is she wants to say to the surrogates.

At the eighth session, the daughter pours out her apology. She begs forgiveness. The surrogates each tell her one at a time that they do forgive her. She is free. The debt is paid.

In Society Four, which not only values forgiving but also makes it easier to accomplish, isolation gives way to reconnection. Offended people and offenders are encouraged to search for the roots from which they may have been severed in a terrible injury. What would happen, though, if everyone forgave everyone? Could there be a *too forgiving* society?

The major fear associated with too much forgiveness—whether it is an individual's fear or a society's fear—is that forgiveness invites repeated offense. Some may even fear that forgiveness invites evil. If a person or a society lets down its guard and slackens its vigilance, some think, injury will surely follow. (This fear is central to the fear of neo-Nazism.) When it is evil or repeated offense that is feared, those who are afraid should remember that real forgiveness does not come about easily. As the interviewees made clear, there are prices to pay: hatred, punishment, and promises.

If forgiveness is granted to someone who feels no contrition or who is seeking to manipulate another person by being forgiven, then it might be dangerous; but it is also not true forgiveness. Or if a person claims to forgive and forgive but is actually using the "forgiveness" to control other people, again it is not true forgiveness. Manipulative "forgivers" who use the language of forgiveness to weave sticky webs of obligation around those they "forgive" can also be dangerous. They use a tool of peacemaking to gain control or power over others.

What about the common situation in which the injurer or injured is absent? If uninvolved parties like the surrogates in Society Four forgave injuries, could forgiveness be dangerous? The answer again lies in the validity of the contrite feelings of the person seeking to be forgiven.

If people confess to helpers or priests or other third parties solely to be relieved of blame or responsibility for hurting someone, then forgiveness is not what they seek. They seek pardoning in order to be relieved of any debt or responsibility to those they have harmed. Too much pardoning could be dangerous. There are responsibilities toward those people whom one unforgivably injures. Surrogate forgiving does not take those away.

It is likely, then, that a society could not endanger itself by being too forgiving. Forgiveness does not release an offender from being punished. A society could perhaps be too pardoning or condoning and endanger itself—a highly unlikely prospect, however.

Forgiveness in the Real World

Our society is not like any of the hypothetical societies. It is a blend of them all. In our society, forgiveness and nonforgiveness spill over us just as they do in mythical societies, but to different degrees.

In America, some people continue to live near those who hurt them. They might avoid their injurers at all costs or erect psychological defenses against them. The rigidities and vigilance of these kinds of nonforgivers must, in some small way, affect the rest of us.

Some people might move across the country from those they injure, severing all ties. Their rootlessness and superficial bonds must, in some small way, affect the rest of us.

Some people retaliate against those who harm them. Their craftiness and violence must, in some small way, affect the rest of us. However, no matter how we affect each other by our harbored resentments and hatreds, our society is one that has many barriers to forgiveness. Even the interviewees, whose horrible damage drove them toward forgiveness more than lesser injuries might, had difficulty overcoming the barriers to forgiving. How can we remove some of the obstacles and make forgiving an easier objective?

BARRIER ONE: MAKING A PRIVATE WOUND A LEGAL
MATTER

Since so many unforgivable injuries are also legal matters, they often
lead to adversarial proceedings in courts of law. Divorces, contested
wills, and sexual assaults, each described by interviewees as unforgivable, are also the material for ugly lawsuits. While many harmed
interviewees were still in the grips of the moral damage and the
unraveling of trust and love their injuries precipitated, they were
counseled by their attorneys to do what is not natural after harm
occurs. They were counseled not to talk about the injury with the
injurer.

Attorneys fear that admission of wrongdoing or apologies can be
later used as evidence in lawsuits between harmers and harmed. But
it is the admission of wrongdoing and/or apology that also initiates
the process of forgiving between two people. An apology is an invitation to discussion. It is also a way to restore some power to a
wounded person. After someone hears an apology, he can condemn
the injurer, demand changes, or try to understand why the person
did what he did. Then, if he chooses, he can forgive. He can also,
as attorneys fear, sue the apologizer and use the apology against the
injurer.

When private unforgivable injuries too quickly become legal matters, that which might serve to begin the process of forgiveness, an
apology, is forbidden. As divorce proceedings or other actions "heat
up," people who have been lovers or friends, husbands and wives,
all too quickly find that they are litigants and adversaries. The unique
moral history woven by two people who once cared for each other
can cease abruptly in the hateful atmosphere of a courtroom before
people can assess what has happened to them. Their complex feelings
for each other can be quickly reduced to hate as the quarreling over
financial arrangements and material possessions reduces parents,
friends, and partners to spiteful adversaries. Once people have been
reduced to their basest selves, even if they might have wanted to
apologize, they may never be willing to do so again. Without confes-
sions of wrongdoing or apologies, forgiveness *between* two people

will not occur. Just as the interviewees forgave their absent harmers, though, those who never hear an apology *can* forgive; but in all likelihood they, too, will have to do it alone.

To overcome the barrier to forgiveness that is erected when unforgivable harms become legal matters, it might be wise for people to wait before they take their problems into the courtroom. Perhaps people should seek counseling first. Society might provide "cool off" counseling, or harmed people might seek it for themselves before they unwittingly let the confused emotions they feel toward the injurer turn into concrete hatred. The adversarial nature of the litigious society in which we live has, for many people, reduced their most complex and precious relationships to simple, single-issue ruin. The mercy of forgiveness *can* occur side by side with legal justice, but it may be much more difficult to accomplish if legal action has destroyed the possibility of apology.

BARRIER TWO: BAD HELP

Many interviewees—as many as were engaged in legal action—also sought help from professionals. Most often they got bad help.

Helping professionals and clergy have preconceived ideas, as we all do, about right and wrong, moral contracts, and, particularly, what is forgivable or unforgivable. One of the worst experiences that can confront a wounded person is for a professional helper to dismiss his injury or minimize its importance. Another is for the helper to believe deeply that the injury the client wants to forgive should never be forgiven. When an unforgivably injured person looks for help, he wants to know that the helper understands the reasons he believes he was unforgivably hurt. He wants the helper to place no negative value on forgiveness.

It is perfectly justifiable for a person seeking help to ask two questions of a professional: "Do you believe that injuries like this one are unforgivable?" and "Are you afraid of rage; can I express it here?"

Because working through unforgivable wounds is a process filled with rage, the professional should be able to help the client confront it and manage it. If clients and professionals are working toward different objectives—for example, if a client wants to forgive and a therapist does not believe he should—then the therapeutic process can be very unhelpful. Clients and helping professionals should openly clarify their thoughts about forgiveness, and a wounded person should feel free to shop around until he finds a professional who has the same ideas about forgiving that he has.

Forgiving is difficult enough to accomplish when it goes smoothly. It is even harder if a trusted "helper" is opposed to it.

BARRIER THREE: FRIENDS AND FAMILY MEMBERS

For the interviewees, friends were most often the major source of support whenever help with forgiveness was offered. Friends often attempted to help people alter the "black and white" thinking about offenders that injured people can fall prey to. But friends and family, like helping professionals, can have some immutable values about retribution and forgiveness.

When people are hurt, it is difficult for those who love them not to feel their pain. If friends do not believe in forgiving and also feel the injured person's pain, they might want, as much as the wounded person, to get even with the harmer.

Our society has an odd relationship with retribution and violence. Friends are as affected by society's ambivalence about violence as most people are. Most religions, for example, speak out strongly against violence, yet many of those same religions support war if it is waged for the "right" cause. Community leaders, politicians, and clergy may rail against violence in the streets, yet violence in the streets is a major theme of television and film entertainment and nightly news.

The friends and family members of unforgivably wounded people are subject to the same desires to retaliate against intrusive harms as anyone else. They are also part of a society that is confused about revenge, retribution, and retaliation.

No one has the "right" answer about when a person should, or should not, forgive. When friends or family members who do not believe in forgiving become obstacles to the forgiveness process, a harmed person should be prepared to help the friend to see that each person must deal with his injuries in his own way. Forgiveness truly does belong to the injured and to no one else. No one can do it for anyone else, and no one should try to stop another from accomplishing it. The wounded should also understand, though, that their nonforgiveness has affected those who love them. It has contaminated their friendships and family relations. Thus, when a person finally makes the choice to forgive, he may want to give special thanks to those who have shared his grief and rage and ask them also to share his forgiveness.

Friends and families are among the greatest promoters of forgiving. They are supports, assets, and gifts that help forgivers regain their resources. When they become barriers to forgiveness, they should be valued just the same. They have their own burdens to carry.

BARRIER FOUR: NOT KNOWING HOW TO FORGIVE

It might be an easier task to forgive if people could observe how role models accomplish forgiveness. If community leaders, politicians, and educators publicly demonstrated some of the elements of forgiving, others might be able to follow suit. The elements of forgiving—admitting wrongdoing, apologizing, making and keeping promises, and showing contrition when a person hurts someone—are noble acts. They are paradoxical by nature, because the person who admits wrongness, or the admission, gives power to those he has offended.

If a corporate president called his stockholders together and admitted he lied about the stock portfolio; or if a cheating wife called her husband to the kitchen to confess an affair; or if a cheater at school approached his teacher to admit the cheating, each would thereby shift the balance of power from himself to the person he cheated. The stockholders could demand that the CEO step down. The husband could leave the cheating wife and take their assets with him. The teacher could punish the student.

Still, most people are able to recognize the grace and nobility of a person's admitting when he has been wrong. To witness true contrition from a person who has hurt another is to witness the essence of the conscience in action.

Where do we see public apologies? We are more likely to hear a fish sing than a politician publicly apologize. It may be the same for businessmen, clergy, doctors, and teachers. In a sense, a society in which it has become inelegant or even foolish to admit wrongdoing is a society whose morality is off course.* If the admission of wrongdoing has become passé, it might follow that contrition for wrongdoing will become an equally quaint notion.

Our leaders may be wise to recognize that public admissions of wrongness open up the doors to the rest of us to do the same.

Television and motion pictures might benefit us if they refrained from presenting such an excess of material where the harming of human beings is done without either apology or emotion. Other media, such as those that falsely accuse or reveal personal matters of people who cannot defend themselves, might curtail their harmfulness or issue apologies to those they wound. Such actions would garner the respect of countless people.

If role models and leaders of all kinds would demonstrate that it is still incorrect to harm others with impunity and, conversely, noble to take responsibility for the harm one does, we might all benefit.

Eight Everyday Activities Toward a More Forgiving Society

No one person can change society, especially those aspects of society that present barriers to forgiveness.

Our society is mobile. Injurers are able to escape those they injure. We are competitive. It has become easy for people to regard others

* There have been several recent reports about our society's moral breakdown—increases in cheating of all kinds, doctors' lying to patients, and people's willingness to falsify such personal documents as résumés, for example.

as foes. We are litigious. It may be simpler to reduce the complex nature of an injurious intimate relationship to a simple victim/victimizer dichotomy. Society *is* violent, and most people view violence with some ambivalence. Our leaders think that they must be infallible, many apparently believing that the graciousness of an apology will be confused with weakness.

None of us can single-handedly alter the "big picture." People can change their own lives, however. Anyone can demonstrate that he wants the ripple effects of unchecked hatred and nonforgiveness to stop at his own doorstep. Anyone can bring some small measure of peace to his own circle of family and friends, even if there is little else he can do.

Here are eight everyday activities anyone can do to promote forgiveness:

1. Admit when you are wrong speedily and openly.
2. Apologize to people you have wronged. If possible, issue your apology in the presence of others to demonstrate that you are not afraid to return power to those you have hurt.
3. Praise those close to you when they express regret about hurting someone. Encourage them to admit wrongdoing and apologize to the injured person.
4. Respect the attempts of others to forgive someone.
5. When it is true, tell people who have modeled forgiveness to you that you respect their achievements. By the same token, when other people's nonforgiveness contaminates you, tell them.
6. Avoid litigation until you have heard each other's views of the injury. Forgiveness is more likely when people are not adversaries.
7. Teach that life is not fair. One person will have more gifts and opportunities than another person and fewer than others. Envy or greed should never be the basis of nonforgiveness.
8. To forgive is to choose to move forward into the future. Show others that you choose the future, not the past, as the focus of aspirations in your daily life.

If none of us ever forgave, it is clear, we would all feel the effects of nonforgiveness. Fortunately, some people can accomplish forgiveness even in the face of formidable obstacles. Overcoming obstacles to forgiving is as much an individual achievement as forgiving is. Forgiving is a profoundly personal journey.

We might be able to make it easier for each other to forgive, though. We could make it clear to each other when we feel bad for hurting others. We could admit wrongdoing, apologize, and show that we value the reconciliatory power of forgiveness as much as we value the material redistribution that justice brings.

Forgiveness is one of the only forms of freedom that any person can give to another. A poor person can forgive. A child can forgive. Old people can forgive. It is one freeing art that anyone, regardless of race, age, or material well-being, can choose to give another while he, at the same time, returns freedom to his own life.

If society has erected barriers to forgiving, each of us can tear one down, if only a little, by removing our contribution to it. After all, we, collectively, are society. Our society's relationship with violence, greed, and envy is in the hands of each of us to shape. Each of us will also, in our own small way, help to shape the future of forgiveness. The sculpture of it all—greed and apathy, compassion and kindness—makes us who we are. How each of us acts toward one another today will be our small contribution to forgiveness in the future. Surely a future where there is no forgiveness is too awful to contemplate.

NOTES

INTRODUCTION

1. D. Droll, "Forgiveness: Theory and Research" (Ph.D. diss., University of Nevada–Reno, April 1984), p. 83; H.J.N. Horsbrugh, "Forgiveness," *Canadian Journal of Philosophy* 4, no. 2 (December 1974), 269–82; J. C. Lampert, "The Human Action of Forgiving: A Critical Application of the Metaphysics of Alfred North Whitehead" (Ph.D. diss., Columbia University, 1980), pp. 63–65; J. A. Martin, "A Realistic Theory of Forgiveness," in *The Return to Reason*, ed. J. Wild (Chicago: Henry Regnery, 1953), pp. 313–32; J. W. Scott. "Idealism and the Conception of Forgiveness," *International Journal of Ethics* 21 (January 1911): 189–98.

2. H. Arendt, *The Human Condition* (Chicago: University of Chicago Press, 1958), p. 274; R. S. Downie, "Forgiveness," *Philosophical Quarterly* 15 (1965): 128–34: Martin, "Theory of Forgiveness," pp. 326–27.

3. Horsbrugh, "Forgiveness," p. 279; Lampert, "Whitehead," p. 64.

4. H. Morris, *On Guilt and Innocence* (Berkeley: University of California Press, 1976), pp. 44–45, 103–10; L. Morrow, "I Spoke as a Brother," *Time*, 9 January 1984, pp. 27–33; Downie, "Forgiveness," p. 131.

5. Downie, "Forgiveness," p. 131; Morrow, "I Spoke as a Brother," pp. 29–30.

6. Downie, "Forgiveness," p. 131.

7. Martin, "Theory of Forgiveness," pp. 313–32; Morris, *On Guilt and Innocence*. pp. 105–10.

8. Martin, "Theory of Forgiveness," pp. 323–24.

9. Lampert, "Whitehead," p. 64.

10. P. Twamley, "Mercy and Forgiveness," *Analysis* 36 (1976): 84–90.

CHAPTER 1

1. J. A. Martin, "A Realistic Theory of Forgiveness," in *The Return to Reason*, ed. J. Wild (Chicago: Henry Regnery, 1953), pp. 313–32.

2. Aristotle, *Nichomachean Ethics*, Books 8 and 9 (Indianapolis: Liberal Arts Press, 1962), pp. 214–72; R. S. Downie, "Forgiveness," *Philosophical Quarterly* 15 (1986): 128–34; Martin, "Theory of Forgiveness," pp. 315–18; H. Morris, *On Guilt and Innocence* (Berkeley: University of California Press, 1976), pp. 89–110.

3. Martin, "Theory of Forgiveness," p. 315.

CHAPTER 2

1. J. H. Harvey, G. L. Wells, and M. D. Alvarez, "Attribution in the Context of Conflict and Separation in Close Relationships," in *New Directions in Attribution Research*, vol. 2, eds. J. Harvey, W. Ickes, and R. F. Kidd (Hillsdale, N.J.: Lawrence Erlbaum Associates, 1978), pp. 235–60.

2. For further references regarding the moral development of children, see M. L. Hoffman, "Power Assertion by the Parent and Its Impact on the Child," *Child Development* 31 (1960): 129–43; L. Kolberg, *The Philosophy of Moral Development* (New York: Harper & Row, 1981); J. Piaget, *The Moral Judgment of the Child* (New York: Free Press, 1965).

3. M. L. Hoffman, "Conscience, Personality, and Socialization Techniques," *Human Development* 13 (1970): 90–126; P. Mussen and N. Eisenberg-Berg, *Roots of Caring, Sharing, and Helping* (San Francisco: W. H. Freeman, 1977), pp. 74–108; Piaget, *Moral Judgment*, p. 295.

4. Piaget, *Moral Judgment*, p. 295.

CHAPTER 3

1. A. Alvarez, *Life After Marriage* (New York: Simon & Schuster, 1981), p. 174.

2. M. Bard and D. Sangrey, *The Crime Victim's Book* (New York: Basic Books, 1979), pp. 40–45.

3. P. Chodoff, D. Friedman, and D. Hamburg, "Stress Defenses and Coping Behaviors: Observations in Parents of Children with Malignant Disease," *American Journal of Psychiatry* 120 (1964): 743–49; Bard and Sangrey, *Crime Victim's Book*, p. 40.

CHAPTER 4

1. Cause, duration, controllability, and consequences are extracted from the Common Sense model. This model is an information-processing paradigm identifying the way people construct meaning for body sensations. See H. Leventhal, D. Meyer, and D. Nerenz, "The Common Sense Representation of Illness Danger," in *Contributions to Medical Psychology*, vol. 2, ed. S. Rachman (New York: Pergamon Press, 1980), pp. 7–30.

2. M. J. Lerner, D. T. Miller, and J. G. Holmes, "Deserving and the Emergence of Forms of Justice," in *Advances in Experimental Social Psychology*, vol. 9, eds. L. Berkowitz and E. Walster (New York: Academic Press, 1976), pp. 133–62; see also M. L. Lerner, in *An Introduction to Attribution Processes*, ed. K. G. Shaver (Cambridge, Mass.: Winthrop Publishers, 1975), pp. 106–7.

3. D. Droll, "Forgiveness: Theory and Research" (Ph.D. diss, University of Nevada–Reno, April 1984); J. H. Harvey, G. L. Wells, and M. D. Alvarez, "Attribution in the Context of Conflict and Separation in Close Relationships," in *New Directions in Attribution Research*, vol. 2, eds. J. Harvey, W. Ickes, and R. F. Kidd (Hillsdale, N.J.: Lawrence Erlbaum Associates, 1978), pp. 235–60.

4. C. Riordan, N. Marlin, and K. Kellogg, "The Effectiveness of Accounts Following Transgressions," *Social Psychology Quarterly* 46, no. 3 (1983): 213–19.

5. B. Orvis, H. H. Kelley, and D. Butler, "Attribution Conflict in Young Couples," in *New Directions in Attribution Research*, vol. 1, eds. J. Harvey, W. Ickes, and R. F. Kidd (Hillsdale, N.J.: Lawrence Erlbaum Associates, 1976), pp. 166–82.

6. Droll, "Forgiveness: Theory," p. 61.

7. H. Braiker and H. H. Kelley, "Conflict in the Development of Close Relationships," in *Social Exchange in Developing Relationships*, eds. R. Burgess and T. Huston (New York: Academic Press, 1979), pp. 24–33.

8. R. S. Weiss, *Marital Separation* (New York: Basic Books, 1975), pp. 10–19; Harvey, Wells, and Alvarez, "Conflict and Separation," pp. 236–52.

9. Harvey, Wells, and Alvarez, "Conflict and Separation," pp. 236–55.

CHAPTER 6

1. K. G. Shaver, *The Attribution of Blame: Causality, Responsibility, and Blameworthiness* (New York: Springer-Verlag, 1985).

2. J. A. Martin, "A Realistic Theory of Forgiveness," in *The Return to Reason*, ed. J. Wild (Chicago: Henry Regnery, 1953), p. 322; H. Morris, *On Guilt and Innocence* (Berkeley: University of California Press, 1976), pp. 60–61.

3. Morris, *On Guilt and Innocence*, pp. 60–63.

4. For a discussion of Fritz Heider's pioneering work on levels of personal responsibility, see K. G. Shaver, *An Introduction to Attribution Processes*, (Cambridge, Mass: Winthrop Publishing Co., 1975), pp. 39–44.

5. Shaver, *Attribution of Blame*, pp. 110–35.

6. W. Ickes and M. A. Layden, "Attributional Styles," in *New Directions in Attributional Research*, vol. 2, eds. J. Harvey, W. Ickes, and R. F. Kidd (Hillsdale, N.J.: Lawrence Erlbaum Associates, 1978), pp. 119–52.

7. Shaver, *Attribution of Blame*, pp. 80–89; Ickes and Layden, "Attributional Styles," pp. 131–52.

CHAPTER 7

1. For a discussion of balance in relationships and some recent arguments against the concept, see P. Watzlawick, *Pragmatics of Human Communication* (New York: W. W. Norton, 1967); S. Minuchin, *Families and Family Therapy* (Cambridge, Mass.: Harvard University Press, 1974); L. von Bertalanffy, *General System Theory* (New York: George Braziller, 1969); and H. Chubb, "Looking at Systems as Process," *Family Process* 29, no. 2 (June 1990): 169–75.

2. P. Watzlawick, J. H. Weakland, and R. Fisch, *Change: Principles of Problem Formation and Problem Resolution* (New York: W. W. Norton, 1974).

3. S. Bok, *Lying—Moral Choice in Public and Private Life* (New York: Vintage Books, 1979), pp. 19–33; C. Fried, *Right and Wrong* (Cambridge, Mass.: Harvard University Press, 1978), pp. 62–69.

4. J. A. Martin, "A Realistic Theory of Forgiveness," in *The Return to Reason*, ed. J. Wild (Chicago: Henry Regnery, 1953), p. 323.

5. A. von Hirsch, *Doing Justice—The Choice of Punishments* (New York: Hill and Wang, 1976), pp. 47, 161; B. Schwartz, "Vengeance and For-

giveness: The Uses of Beneficence in Social Control," *School Review* (August 1978): 655–68; Martin, "Theory of Forgiveness," p. 324.

6. von Hirsch, *Doing Justice*, p. 161.

7. For a discussion of Immanuel Kant's theory of punishment, see von Hirsch, *Doing Justice*, pp. 46–48. Kant argued that those who disregard moral rules take advantage of others. Thus, a person who infringes on another's rights does wrong, benefits himself, and should subsequently be blamed and finally punished. Punishment rectifies balance, according to Kant.

8. Martin, "Theory of Forgiveness," pp. 323–24; H. Morris, *On Guilt and Innocence* (Berkeley: University of California Press, 1976), pp. 104–5.

9. von Hirsch, *Doing Justice*; Martin, "Theory of Forgiveness."

CHAPTER 9

1. The term *cognitive dissonance* was introduced by Leon Festinger in his book *A Theory of Cognitive Dissonance* (Stanford, Calif.: Stanford University Press, 1957). Since that time, the concept has gained wide acceptance by researchers and helping professionals.

CHAPTER 12

1. For a discussion of styles of fixing responsibility, see the work of Martin, E. P. Seligman, and colleagues. Seligman and others have developed the Attribution Style Questionnaire (ASQ), which has been administered to various kinds of research subjects to measure explanatory styles. See specifically Robert J. Trotter, "Stop Blaming Yourself," *Psychology Today* 21, no. 2 (February 1987): 31–39.

CHAPTER 13

1. R. S. Madara and A. Meese, eds. *The Self-Help Sourcebook: Finding and Forming Mutual Aid Self-Help Groups.* (Danville, N.J.: New Jersey Self-Help Clearinghouse, St. Clares—Riverside Medical Center, 1986).

CHAPTER 16

1. E. Becker, *The Denial of Death.* (New York: Free Press, 1973), p. 150.

INDEX

ABOUT THE AUTHOR

Beverly Flanigan, M.S.S.W., is a Clinical Professor at the School of Social Work, University of Wisconsin, and a therapist in private practice. As a Fellow of the Kellogg Foundation, she conducted the first in-depth study of forgiveness and devised a model of the six-phase process of forgiving. She has written and lectured widely on the subject and conducted numerous seminars and workshops with both professional and lay audiences. She lives in Madison, Wisconsin.